The Manager as Facilitator

Recent Titles in
The Manager as ...

The Manager as Facilitator

Judy Whichard and Nathalie L. Kees

The Manager as …
Jerry W. Gilley, Series Editor

Westport, Connecticut
London

Library of Congress Cataloging-in-Publication Data

Whichard, Judy.
    The manager as facilitator / Judy Whichard and Nathalie L. Kees.
        p. cm. — (The manager as—)
    Includes bibliographical references and index.
    ISBN 0–275–98985–2
    1. Management—Handbooks, manuals, etc. 2. Group facilitation—
Handbooks, manuals, etc. I. Kees, Nathalie L. II. Title. III. Series.
HD38.15.W54   2006
658.4—dc22   2006007250

British Library Cataloguing in Publication Data is available.

Library of Congress Catalog Card Number: 2006007250

ISBN: 0–275–98985–2

ISSN: 1555–7480

First published in 2006

Praeger Publishers, 88 Post Road West, Westport, CT 06881
An imprint of Greenwood Publishing Group, Inc.
www.praeger.com

Printed in the United States of America

The paper used in this book complies with the
Permanent Paper Standard issued by the National
Information Standards Organization (Z39.48–1984).

10   9   8   7   6   5   4   3   2   1

Contents

Publisher's Note

The backbone of every organization, large or small, is its managers. They guide and direct employees' actions, decisions, resources, and energies. They serve as friends and leaders, motivators and disciplinarians, problem solvers and counselors, partners and directors. Managers serve as liaisons between executives and employees, interpreting the organization's mission and realizing its goals. They are responsible for performance improvement, quality, productivity, strategy, and execution—through the people who work for and with them. All too often, though, managers are thrust into these roles and responsibilities without adequate guidance and support. MBA programs provide book learning but little practical experience in the art of managing projects and people; at the other end of the spectrum, exceptional talent in one's functional area does not necessarily prepare the individual for the daily rigors of supervision. This series is designed to address those gaps directly.

The Manager as ... series provides a unique library of insights and information designed to help managers develop a portfolio of outstanding skills. From Mentor to Marketer, Politician to Problem Solver, Coach to Change Leader, each book provides an introduction to the principles, concepts, and issues that define the role; discusses the evolution of recent and current trends; and guides readers through the dynamic process of assessing their strengths and weaknesses and creating a personal development plan. Featuring diagnostic tools, exercises, checklists, case examples, practical tips, and recommended resources, the books in this series will help readers at any stage in their careers master the art and science of management.

Introduction

Talented employees need great managers.[1]

Effective managers are central assets of successful organizations. Regardless of attractive compensation packages, promised promotions, and first-rate training opportunities, companies without good managers simply do not attract and retain talented employees. In fact, employee productivity and tenure with companies is directly proportionate to the extent of their positive relationships with immediate supervisors.[2] For their part, good managers adroitly juggle art and science—balancing humanism with corporate bottom lines, assessing individual strengths and challenges, negotiating with equally capable colleagues for limited resources, moving forward to meet deadlines, and stepping back to regroup—all the while mindful of motivating their employees to meet or exceed organizational aspirations and expectations.

In today's highly competitive world of work, effectively managing employees is an often daunting challenge. Workplace stress levels are fueled by a number of factors to an unprecedented extent. Employees are expected to meet higher and faster productivity rates with fewer resources. Profitable bottom lines mean continually growing market share despite soaring global competition. As workers now shop for employment options worldwide, retaining qualified employees is progressively more difficult. Technology has become an expensive necessity that quickly becomes obsolete and drains fiscal resources. All in all, employees are asked to work in unstable work environments with limited resources under the ongoing threat of job loss.

Acknowledging the complexities of effective management, this book is intended as an off-the-shelf, functional, straightforward resource to help managers, supervisors, organizational change agents, and consultants interact most effectively with their colleagues and employees in accomplishing organizational tasks. Its purpose is to equip these individuals with proven tools and techniques that build and guide individuals, small and large groups, and the larger organization toward developing their fullest potential while achieving corporate goals.

For ease of usage, the book chapters all follow a similar format, beginning with a content overview followed by a presentation and discussion of main themes. Each chapter ends with a summary of key points and chapter implications. Throughout the book, we provide assessment tools and questionnaires for gaining insights into both individual and team dynamics.

Because our philosophies of management are a cornerstone of this book, we are including a brief discussion of our ideas and beliefs. Informed by both academic study and practical professional experience, we have identified what we think are common characteristics of effective managers. The following list is not meant to be exhaustive or to neglect the uniqueness of management style; it is rather a summarization of factors that we have noted in managers who time and again meet organizational goals while earning the esteem of their employees.

- Managers are *clear about their managerial purpose* and role. They know what the organization expects from them and how the organization expects them to perform their roles. Moreover, they assume ultimate responsibility for executing their roles.
- Managers operate from a *basis of personal principles*. They strive for integrity in all of their decisions and actions, insist on ethical conduct in all professional and personal interactions, and consistently align words with behaviors.
- Managers are responsible for *keeping a disciplined focus on the organizational mission* and for ensuring that their and their employees' actions consistently reflect this mission.
- Managers are *genuinely concerned about the welfare* of their employees. They practice honest and open communication, are good listeners, suspend judgment until all facts are gathered, are accessible and inclusive, and are fair in employee assessments. They empower their employees and trust them to make important decisions.

- Managers *are sensitive to and respectful of diversity*. They strive to understand and accommodate employees' differing needs, styles, and perspectives as appropriate.
- Managers *set and maintain team parameters*. They exemplify effective team-building and team-operating behaviors.
- Managers understand and *use both their human and material resources wisely*. They take every opportunity to learn about and take advantage of their employees' talents and strengths, and they monitor resource-use efficiency.
- Managers know how to *procure the necessary resources* that enable their employees to successfully complete their responsibilities.
- Managers *are adaptable*. They assess situations quickly, identify needed modifications, and adjust plans accordingly.
- Managers *assume responsibility for the ongoing education/training* of themselves and their employees.

These attributes include some of the key behaviors shared by effective managers with whom we have worked and were initially included only to give readers a glimpse of our thinking. Yet the more we reviewed these attributes the more we realized that the majority of them were also attributes associated with proficient facilitation. Our conclusion is that as managers acquire greater facilitation skills they enhance and hone other leadership skills as well.

Today's accomplished managers must be facilitators in the broadest sense of the word—they are the pivotal force behind tapping into and focusing individual and group expertise on successfully completing the tasks at hand. They are responsible for assessing and developing their employees' talents and creating and maintaining a work environment that brings these talents to fruition. Managers must relentlessly pursue productive employee interactions, encouraging open discussion and debate while minimizing harmful conflict. They need to establish work groups or teams that are independent, yet responsive to and in tune with larger corporate goals. Employee commitment and loyalty to their employers is critical to organizational success, and managers are relied on to foster both. In short, managers are responsible for the most fundamental aspect of business success—finding and keeping talented, productive, positive, and innovative employees. To realize this, they must be good facilitators.

This book will help managers, supervisors, change agents, and consultants develop and practice strong facilitation skills. Through these facilitation skills, managers and others should be able to create a climate of employee well-being and industry; focus employee talents on accomplishing organizational goals with minimal setbacks; inspire employee creativity and innovation; increase overall productivity; and foster employee fidelity and commitment to the organization.

As to the importance of employee loyalty and its role in successfully completing organizational tasks, consider the following from Thomas Stewart in *Intellectual Capital:* "the most essentially human tasks: sensing, judging, creating, and building relationships."[3] are the most valuable aspects of today's jobs. Today, when someone leaves a company, she takes her value with her—more often than not to the competition. Successful companies, consequently, realize that finding and keeping talented employees is more than honing their competitive edge—it is often a matter of survival. Reviewed under this light, facilitation may well be a managerial imperative.

ONE

The Evolving Managerial Role

What employees and managers ask from a company is that they get a chance to contribute something ... that their efforts amount to something and [are] recognized. When this is provided to them, their loyalty is cemented and their performance remains solid.[1]

Rapid change and revolutionary discoveries constantly reshape our world. Increased sophistication of and reliance on technology, burgeoning economic globalization, and borderless "cyber" communication systems presents with more information than we can assimilate. Greeting us at every turn, complex and highly diverse possibilities and problems demand attention and quick resolution. Savvy consumers "shop" worldwide, creating unprecedented competition for quality goods and services. Highly mobile, educated workers, loyal to their ideas and skills rather than employers, are the growing norm.

In the workplace, these forces present both exciting possibilities and monumental challenges. As trends evolve, businesses are compelled to learn and relearn strategies to ensure a company's competitive advantage. More and more of these strategies involve the effective recruitment and management of employees. Typically this translates into managers playing an amplified role in the daily routines and lives of their employees while assuming greater strategic importance in the overall organization.

ORGANIZATIONAL TRENDS

In this chapter, we provide information on how and why American organizations are rethinking how they perform "business as usual." We speak to some of the major changes in organizational thinking and cover some of the primary implications for managers. We define facilitation and its components. In subsequent chapters, we provide greater detail on how managers can facilitate the sustained satisfaction and effectiveness of their employees. As we have learned, managers wear multiple hats as they pilot the twists and turns of contemporary managerial highways and byways.

Organizations Are No Longer Perceived as Rational Entities

Traditionally, business schools carefully developed their management students' "strategic skills." Graduates were able to manipulate and rely on numbers for making sound decisions—calculating risk and opportunity costs, gauging their competitors' advantages, navigating the world of high finance, and predicting the bottom line. The underlying premise for the "strategic manager" rests on the lofty shoulders of experimentation and mathematics: Business is a rational process and irrationality happens only when something has gone awry. Therefore, business will prosper when its operations are logical and controlled.

The rapid pace of today's competitive world coupled with a better understanding of employee satisfaction underscores how passé such tenets have become. To keep their competitive edge, businesses need to keep abreast of many events very quickly. Employees with the ability to think independently and share their findings are the single best solution for ensuring corporate competitiveness. Unpredictability is a given, and the best way to address it is through engaged, empowered employees with heartfelt commitment to the organization rather than relying on outdated operations manuals and indisputable, hierarchical protocols.

Mechanistic Business Models Are Obsolete

Working hand in hand with the "business is rational" model, mechanistic methods presume that efficiency and thus greater productivity is achieved through "human engineering." Such methods focus on eliminating unnecessary motion and "downtime" by cutting out the human factors (for example, mistakes, absences, diverse thinking). Employees are pigeonholed, behavioral and performance strategies are centrally and hierarchically imposed and managed, and employees are reduced to mechanically repetitive jobs with the idea that repetition yields resourceful perfection. In such settings, employees and managers alike are deprived of intrinsic motivation and passion.

Not only does this approach ignore the spontaneous complexity of our world, but it also disregards what we've learned about business's competitive advantage. When employees are encouraged to exercise their creativity and vision freely, organizations realize greater innovations and productivity. Currently, organizations attempting to be humanistic, fair, moral, and reasonable are those with the greatest probability of engendering employee commitment, enthusiasm, and creative energy.[2]

The Concept of Productivity Has Changed

As evidenced by the waning number of low-wage, low-skill jobs, businesses have shifted away from the "assembly line" mentality. More often than not, organizations look for well-educated, independent thinkers who are adept at lifelong learning. Today's employees need to perform at higher levels of intellect and judgment, particularly as their outcomes grow more important to the organization's success. Unlike traditional position descriptions that expected more insular employee performances, employees now decide independently almost moment by moment how they can most beneficially accomplish the corporate mission.

For their parts, organizations rely strongly on their employees' judgment, generally paying handsomely for those workers whose decisions boost corporate profits. Productivity is no longer measured chiefly by how much one produces or manufactures or ships each day; rather it is viewed as how much market share the employees' creative, innovative, inspiring ideas purchase. Managers are increasingly called on to initiate and maintain a workplace climate that will maximize their employees' ability to contribute most directly to corporate bottom lines.

Effective Management Is Not Hierarchical

Traditionally, managers worked their way "up the promotion ladder," beginning in the rank and file, moving on to supervisory roles, assuming greater responsibility, and generally following the "party line." Hierarchical in nature, such models usually meant that the higher the management position the more infallible the authority and power. Decisions were made by those at the top with little, if any, consulting with subordinates.

Currently, larger numbers of managers are realizing that autocratic authority and power simply doesn't work with the majority of employees. Employees engaged fully in their work are a company's most critical asset. To become fully engaged, employees need to know where they fit in the overall organization, understand how they uniquely contribute to the organization, and have the freedom and support from their managers to make meaningful decisions and advance innovative ideas. Managers are called upon to facilitate the sustained growth of their employees and encourage their involvement in company operations.

Greater Diversity in the Workplace

Historically, the United States has provided homes to more immigrants than any other country in the world. Today, America is home to many cultures, replete with differing values, lifestyles, attitudes about gender, family life, and so on. A number of religions are scattered across the country, influencing political, economic, social, business, and educational systems. As never before, Americans are faced with overcoming their aversion to differences.

Our various cultures also influence the workplace. Not only does a mixture of cultures compose the American workforce, but its organizations are also progressively more global. Multinational organizations are becoming the norm, forcing workers into varied interactions as a matter of course. Global marketing of goods and services means that familiarity with multiple cultures, complicated at times, is crucial to organizational success. Today's employees must not only acknowledge and accept diversity, they must also value it. Helping facilitate this understanding is one more managerial challenge.

Lifetime Employment Is No Longer Guaranteed

In today's workplace, job security is an anachronism. Competition demands that companies continually initiate new market strategies, meaning people with different skill sets often supplant longtime employees. In addition, technology threatens to replace workers in growing numbers, as does the growing popularity of off-shore outsourcing.

Yet businesses need continuity in their workforce to benefit from the accumulated knowledge their workers possess. This paradox challenges managers to keep employees fully engaged in the business at hand, motivated and committed to the company, while all the while realizing that employment is tenuous.

Money Is Not Always the Key Motivator

Certainly competitive salaries and attractive benefit packages continue to entice talent to an organization. However, with the relative affluence of American workers, money is no longer as strong a lure as it once was. More and more employees are looking for personal satisfaction and significance in the workplace—chiefly, organizational values and virtues that are congruent with their own. Individuals are taking the time to determine how they want to live their lives and are looking for employers who can support their lifestyle choices. They consistently speak about balancing work, family, and leisure (although American workers in general fall short of such balance).[3]

Perhaps most importantly, employee attitudes and lifestyles are shifting away from materialism to human interests and values. Organizations that endorse humanistic management, appreciate the value of family, are environmentally conscientious, practice ethical conduct in all business practices, and are globally aware are those most keenly sought after by prospective employees.[4]

IMPLICATIONS FOR MANAGERS

As we noted initially, a manager's role is growing increasingly complicated. Managers are now assumed to know how to handle a host of responsibilities:

- Identifying the type of workplace in which they are employed, including management structure and organizational values
- Gauging the health of the workplace climate and facilitating remedies when signs of ill health prevail
- Inspiring and motivating their employees despite unstable and stressful workplaces
- Ensuring effective communication among all workers
- Encouraging cultural diversity within a climate of general reluctance to accept differences
- Clarifying individual and corporate roles, purposes, and goals
- Unleashing their employees' creativity and imaginations
- Reflecting organizational ethics and values as well as bring employees "into the fold"
- Meeting organizational productivity goals

In summary, managers, supervisors, change agents, and consultants now are expected to exercise various facilitative roles.

Throughout this book, we will assume that facilitation is the ability to get individuals and groups to accomplish successfully the tasks they are assigned while maintaining integrity, humanism, and compassion in the workplace. This definition only hints about the complexity and importance of facilitation and solid facilitator skills. To help clarify this complexity, Figure 1.1 depicts a model of the various components of facilitation that will be discussed in the remaining chapters. Because organizations are relying more and more on groups to accomplish tasks, each facilitation component as we're presenting it is set within work groups or team settings. However, the components have applicability to numerous workplace situations with both singular and multiple individuals.

Although the remaining chapters will detail each component of the facilitation model, following is a brief overview of each:

- *Facilitating Communication/Conflict Resolution*: opening up and keeping open the lines of communication, including written, oral, and electronic presentations; general sharing of opinions and ideas; identifying and resolving difficult issues arising in the workplace

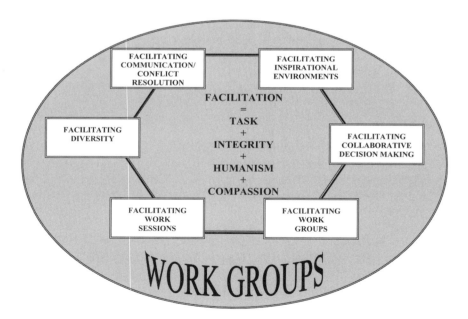

Figure 1.1 Facilitation Model

- *Facilitating Inspirational Environments:* assessing and facilitating a healthy, stimulating climate in the workplace
- *Facilitating Collaborative Decision Making:* encouraging participation in goal setting, workplace operations and problems, and meeting organizational goals
- *Facilitating Work Groups:* building and managing work groups, disbanding them, and identifying group member "roles" and individual member communication preferences and strengths
- *Facilitating Work Sessions:* respecting employees' significance by establishing and running effective meetings and other work sessions
- *Facilitating Diversity:* understanding, encouraging, valuing, and utilizing cultural diversity in the workplace

In the following portions of the book, these facilitation roles are defined and discussed extensively. Methods for acquiring and practicing each role are included, as are assessment tools to help readers determine their present and ongoing progress in developing their facilitative skills. Where helpful, situations describing facilitation in action are included.

One final note: We have used these strategies and have found them effective in achieving our intended facilitation outcomes. Additionally, we know that with practice each can be readily mastered by those considering themselves "facilitator laypersons."

CHAPTER IMPLICATIONS

- As businesses recognize the futility of using mechanistic, hierarchical business models, managers are required to learn about and integrate many human, social, and cultural dimensions into managerial practices.
- Organizations are in continual flux attempting to understand and incorporate rapidly changing global trends into their business practices. Consequently, employees are required to become involved to a greater extent in corporate decision making. Managers are responsible for ensuring that their employees are familiar with and committed to corporate goals.
- More than ever, managers are responsible for recruiting, managing, and retaining talented employees. To do this successfully, they must create and maintain the type of business climate that encourages employee growth, satisfaction, fulfillment, creativity, and imagination. As their employees cope with tenuous employment situations, managers must also be prepared to understand and ameliorate heightened workplace stress.

QUESTIONS FOR REFLECTION

1. How does your organization identify and monitor local, national, and global trends that impact (or potentially could impact) its "bottom line"? Is there a strategy in place for ensuring that such trends are considered when determining daily as well as more long-term operations and goals?

2. What types of business models define your organizational infrastructure? Do they reflect "best practices" for attracting and retaining talent? How does your organization define productivity?

3. To what extent does your organization support your ideas of effective management? Are your superiors' management styles consistent with yours? If different, to what extent are you able to garner their support for your methods and decisions?

TWO

Facilitating Work Groups

A healthy organization always balances the needs and interests of the group with the needs and interests of the individual. [However,] the common good must be held higher than individual gain.[1]

In the 1980s, when business strategists documented that groups created outcomes that were greater than the sum of their respective parts, the term synergy became a buzzword. Since that time, work groups, teams, or strategic units (common labels for the same concept) have become a matter of course. Organizations currently rely on groups for superlative performance in increasing productivity, completing particular projects, or improving organizational processes. However, groups usually don't just happen; to meet organizational expectations groups need to be created, managed, and facilitated effectively. In other words, they need to be taught how to create synergy.

In this chapter, we introduce some "how-tos" of building and managing work groups; provide ways to determine individual members' communication preferences and strengths; discuss the group development process; and give ways to clarify and create a group's charge and charter. Initially, we will speak to the importance of the facilitative role, particularly facilitator self-awareness, and provide ways to develop self-awareness.

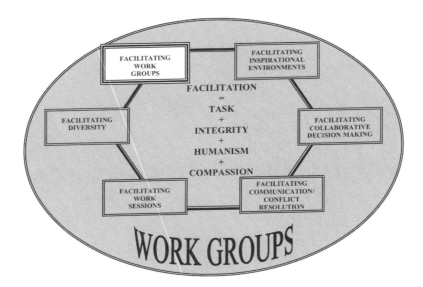

In this chapter, you will learn to:

- Identify your unique values, beliefs, needs, attitudes, and skills about facilitation

- Assess your own and others' temperament styles

- Learn ways to recognize and respond to temperament styles

- Understand the group development process

- Develop a group's charge and charter

FACILITATOR SELF-AWARENESS

Effective facilitators not only have tried-and-true facilitative techniques at their disposal, but also they know how to use themselves to achieve successful groups. They understand themselves intimately and use this knowledge to monitor and establish the "mood" and "nature" of the group as well as of the individual group members.

Reflective self-awareness is the most valuable method of launching successful facilitation. Self-aware facilitators are able to distinguish their thoughts and feelings from those of group members. They accept the members' unique values, beliefs, strengths, needs, attitudes, and skills and understand how they affect facilitation.

Facilitation Values, Beliefs, Needs, Attitudes, and Skills

Values are defined as what individuals consider important. For example, it is important that facilitators value collaborative efforts, honor differences among individuals, and enjoy eliciting meaningful group performances and helping others. *Beliefs* are people's realities—what they believe to be true. Facilitators believe that they are resource gatherers for groups, making it possible for groups to complete their tasks. They believe that accessing individual strengths engages people in meaningful performance and allows groups to operate at their peak. *Needs,* beyond those of basic survival, are what people require to sustain themselves. Group members typically look to the group and its facilitator to satisfy their needs (for example, recognition, social interaction, achievement, stimulation). Facilitators must recognize these needs and the group's ability to satisfy them or face the destructive undercurrents of unmet needs. *Attitudes* are the intellectual or mental perspectives used to make sense of the world and are typically the result of fused values, beliefs, learning, and life experiences. Facilitator attitudes influence the understanding of group interactions and outcomes, as different understandings lead to different facilitative actions.

Facilitators examine carefully the results of their experiences, or those events they've lived through, learning important lessons about what does and doesn't work well in all kinds of situations. They become adept at honing their skills (what they are able to do), focusing on how to garner essential information from group interactions, make timely and meaningful decisions, and subsequently promote further group work.[2] They appreciate that modeling the behaviors they are expecting of group members is indispensable to successful facilitation.

Recognizing Differences in Styles

Developing self-awareness typically begins with self-assessment. We have included a brief history and discussion of temperament theory and the resulting instruments to help both facilitators and the groups they lead gain insights into their living, learning, and working styles. We have used the instruments we mention in various work-related situations and have found each of them useful for helping individuals identify and appreciate their own and others' unique preferences and strengths. Further, each of these instruments has served as points of departure for fruitful discussions on the importance of honoring and encouraging individual differences.

Temperament Theory Overview

As communal beings with strong survival instincts, people have long wondered how they and others experience the world within and around them. For at least 25 centuries, observers of human behavior have been recording major patterns of behaviors. Interestingly, four major behavior patterns have been repeatedly identified. In 450 B.C., Hippocrates described four patterns he named temperaments: a *choleric* temperament that is easily emotionally aroused and sensitive to stimuli; a *phlegmatic* temperament with cool detachment and impassivity; a *melancholic* temperament with a very serious, dour, and downcast nature; and a *sanguine* temperament full of impulsivity, excitability, and quick reactivity. During the Middle Ages, Philippus Paracelsus described four natures whose behaviors were said to be influenced by four kinds of spirits—nymphs, sylphs, gnomes, and salamanders. Paracelsus's work closely mirrored that of Hippocrates.

In the late 1800s and early 1900s, Carl Jung strongly influenced the study of human behaviors by identifying four "archetypes": Feeling Directed, Intellectually Directed, Body Directed, and Intuition Directed. Jung contended that individuals enter the world with a "thumbprint" (a unique combination of the four archetypes with a strong identification with one archetype) that guides them throughout life, defining their very core and determining their life path. Jung was unique in that most twentieth-century psychologists had abandoned holistic observation of human behavior, believing that all human beings were basically alike and that individual differences were due to chance or environmental conditioning. Hence, little work on temperament theory was conducted until the late 1940s and early 1950s.

During World War II, a young woman named Isabel Myers decided to do her part for the war effort by creating a self-report inventory that would make Carl Jung's theory of psychological types available to more people. (At this time only psychologists "assessed" personalities.) Myers's goals were two fold: (1) to help people find a better fit in their work and thus make factory and military efforts more effective; and (2) to promote world peace by helping people develop an appreciation for individual differences and subsequently use their understanding constructively rather than divisively. Her work resulted in worldwide use of the Myers-Briggs Type Indicator (MBTI), spawning an industry of professional "type practitioners" who continue to relate type theory to business effectiveness, communication, career development, cross-cultural understanding, education, spirituality, and more.

Inspired by Jung, Myers, and two early twentieth-century German psychologists, in the 1960s and 1970s psychologist David Keirsey continued to explore the consistent tendency of human behavior to sort itself into four patterns. Using temperament theory instruments based on these four patterns, Keirsey expanded the understanding of how the human personality interacts with the environment to satisfy its needs.

Currently, numerous instruments that assess and measure temperaments are available and share wide use. In addition to Jung's archetypal work and the MBTI, some of the more well known instruments include Linda Berens's Temperament 2–0, the DISC, and David Lowry's True Colors. Their common denominator is four organizing patterns of personality that are based on descriptions of behavior that go back over 25 centuries. The instruments are designed to provide insights into the "whys" of human behavior—our motivators and sources of deep psychological stress. Each advocates that knowing our temperament patterns tells us our core needs and values, as well as the talents we are more likely to develop.

As we have found each useful for enhancing self-awareness, we don't necessarily endorse any one of these temperament theories or their accompanying instruments. We have found great similarity among the theories and instruments (refer to Table 2.1 for a comparison of the instruments we've included), but differences in how they are administered and interpreted. Furthermore, there are many other temperament theory instruments available; the instruments we've discussed are those with which we're most familiar. We encourage you to research and experiment with them to determine those that would be most effective for you and your situation.

In summary, understanding and capitalizing on human preferences is critical in maximizing both individual and group accomplishments. Tools that encourage discovery and appreciation of individual uniqueness have widespread applicability and typically have great benefit for enhancing self-awareness. Moreover, most of the theories and resultant assessment instruments promote similar tenets:

Table 2.1
Temperament Theory Comparison

	Temperament 1	Temperament 2	Temperament 3	Temperament 4
Hippocrates (450 B.C.)	Phlegmatic (Phlegm)	Choleric (Yellow Bile)	Melancholic (Black Bile)	Sanguine (Blood)
Carl Jung Archetypes (1900s)	Feeling Directed	Intellect Directed	Body Directed	Intuition Directed
Myers-Briggs Type Indicator (MBTI) (1950s)	ENFJ INFJ ENFP INFP (NF)	ENTJ INTJ ENTP INTP (NT)	ESTJ ISTJ ESTJ ISFJ (SJ)	ESFP ISFP ESTP ISTP (SP)
David Keirsey (1960-1970s)	Dionysian	Apollonian	Epimethian	Promethian
Linda Berens Temperament 2-0	Idealist	Rational	Guardian	Artisan
DISC	Inducement (I)	Conscientious (C)	Steadiness (S)	Dominance (D)
Don Lowry True Colors (1979)	Blue	Green	Gold	Orange

Note: There is a considerable amount of overlap among these theories and instruments. However, none is perfectly correlated with another.

- Everyone has a preferred style or styles. In learning situations, particularly those that are stressful, people will rely on their preferred style or styles to understand and cope with what is expected of them.
- Everyone is a unique composite of all four styles. Although most individuals exhibit strength in their preferred style or styles, they can be taught to adapt their styles to differing situations.
- People interact with the world through their preferred style or styles. Values and core beliefs spring from their preferences, which dictate their attitudes and behaviors.
- Everyone is seeking validation and self esteem. However, how they find and experience validation and esteem can be quite different.
- Inherent tensions exist among the four styles. As an example, those individuals who prefer order and structure in their world may be "put off" initially by those preferring freedom and independence.
- There is no one right or wrong, better or worse, bad or good style. No style is better than another, although some styles may be more effective in certain situations than others.
- Each style has its strengths and challenges. Every individual has characteristics that are judged as attributes, as well as those that are judged as deficiencies.

Working with Individual Differences

Groups need variety in their members to perform at their best. For example, groups function most effectively and enjoyably when they are composed of some individuals who are particularly adept at analyzing facts and developing systems and some who are sensitive to people's needs and feelings. Order and structure need to be challenged by the freedom to "think outside the box." Timely outcomes need to be tempered by thoughtful group processes that reflect the magnitude and complexity of the task.

Assuming that facilitators have completed an assessment for determining temperaments, they are now prepared to begin examining how their preferences will interface with building work groups. Additionally, they can begin identifying the styles and preferences of work-group members. Table 2.2 provides information about the four predominant styles, giving their natural tendencies as well as their core needs, strengths, and chief motivators.

Typically, individuals exhibit their preferences through their actions, words, and general appearance. However, facilitators need to exercise caution when determining individual preferences. Many behaviors practiced in the workplace are learned; that is to say, individuals have modified their inherent tendencies to accommodate others' expectations. Ideally, facilitators would introduce an assessment instrument at the inception of the group to encourage self-awareness and appreciation of all group members. If this isn't possible, facilitators should observe and monitor individuals' behaviors over time and in multiple situations before deciding their preferences.

As we mentioned earlier, all temperaments have their strengths and challenges. Some natural characteristics foster group facilitation and positive interpersonal relationship, while some can be problematic. Table 2.3 discusses temperament attributes and behaviors and their potential impact when facilitating groups. When assuming the facilitative role, understanding your facilitative tendencies when working with groups is an absolute necessity. Groups respond chiefly to their facilitators' actions and reactions. Thus, facilitators must be able to accurately "read" the effect they are having on the group's development and progress and make any necessary adjustments.

As facilitators become adept at identifying group member temperament preferences, they can begin to interpret better the members' behaviors, emotions, attitudes, and needs. They can become more conscious of their courses of action, choosing interventions and actions that will maximize group success as well as ameliorate problem situations. Tables 2.4 and 2.5 give some additional behavioral cues to the different temperament preferences and offer effective interaction suggestions to facilitators (and work-group members).

Table 2.2
Temperament Attributes

	Temperament 1	Temperament 2	Temperament 3	Temperament 4
They like to be appreciated for:	Unique contributions	Ideas, intelligence	Accuracy, thoroughness	Creativity, cleverness
Their core need is:	Self-actualization	Competency	Social belonging	Freedom
They are esteemed by:	Helping people	Finding insights	Being of service	Recognition
They take pride in:	Their empathy	Their competence	Being dependable	Making an impact
They are stressed by:	Feeling artificial	Inadequacy	Rejection	Restrictions
They strive for and seek from others:	Harmony	Insight	Justice	Independence
They support/foster:	Personal growth	Invention	Institutions	Recreation, fun
They nurture:	A vision of a better world	Technological insights	Helpfulness	Competitiveness
Their specialty is:	Relationships	Strategy	Results	Energy
They trust their:	Intuition	Logic	Authority	Chance
In management, they are:	The catalyst	The visionary	The traditionalist	The troubleshooter
They have intrinsic intelligence:	With people	With strategy	With data	With senses
They become irritated when:	They are treated impersonally	Others become illogical	Others are not using the rules and regulations	They are told how to do things

GROUP INTERACTION AND DEVELOPMENT

Forming functioning work groups has become an essential skill for today's manager. However, business schools only began in the late 1990s to require work-group and team-building strategies in their curricula. Subsequently, many managers have not been involved in programs that teach formal work-group building. The remainder of this chapter will focus on how managers can facilitate the creation and oversight of successful work groups.

Table 2.3
Temperament Facilitation Strengths and Challenges

	Strengths	*Challenges*
Temperament 1	• Enthusiasm • Will include everyone • Sensitive to individual needs • Agreeable demeanor • Charm and poise • Will take some risks • Respectful of self and group members • Honorable motives • Good listener	• May talk too much • May be drawn away from topic easily • May take things personally • May jump to inconsistent conclusions • May become overly emotional
Temperament 2	• Approach problems in a systematic method • Diplomatic in interactions with group members • Will achieve high-quality outcome • Gather data and facts to inform decisions • Calm demeanor	• May withdraw if group deviates from task • May be unwilling to address emotional content • May avoid conflict at all costs • May prefer to work alone • May give preference to data over feelings
Temperament 3	• Patient and quiet demeanor • Persist until goals are reached • Create a predictable group atmosphere • Foster cooperation and team work • Organized and scheduled • Dependable and orderly	• May resist change • May be unwilling to change facilitation style • May have difficulty multitasking • May become upset by open conflict
Temperament 4	• Direct and decisive • Positive and confident • Risk taker • Creative visionary • Energetic • Humorous • Thinks quickly on feet	• May talk too much • May dominate and control the direction and process of groups • May be blunt and sarcastic • May be impatient • May disregard details • May display egotism

Table 2.4
Temperament Behavioral Cues and Interaction Srategies

	What irritates them at work?	*What positively influences them?*
Temperament 1	• Denying their acceptanceand friendship • Isolation • Focusing on the outcome and ignoring the process • Not having their and others' feelings honored • Negativity about their ideas	• Interacting with openness and honesty • Creating a meaningful working atmosphere • Making use of their natural gifts for communication, nurturing, and people-oriented ideas • Treating all group members with dignity and respect • Injecting a personal touch
Temperament 2	• Being asked to do something illogical or without facts • Tedious, nonchallenging tasks • Following rules and regulations that have no relevance or don't make sense • Expecting them to become emotionally involved • Questioning their competence	• Assigning tasks that require their analysis, creativity, and ingenuity • Recognizing (privately) their competence • Providing abundant data • Using diplomacy in interactions • Encouraging independent thinking • Allowing them the freedom to improve systems
Temperament 3	• Decisions not based on policy and procedure • Surprises, especially unexpected changes • Insufficient information about tasks • Not meeting deadlines • Group competition rather than cooperation • Confusion about expectations	• Providing reasons for deviations from policy/procedure • Giving detailed information about assignments and their roles • Giving them time to adjust to changes • Providing timely and sufficient feedback about their progress • Providing follow–up support
Temperament 4	• Being told how to work • Leadership with limited vision and creativity • Routine work • Attacking their character • Inaction	• Allowing them the freedom to perform in their own, often nontraditional, style; encouraging humor • Avoiding routine or boring assignments • Being brief and to the point • Supporting their natural negotiating abilities

Table 2.5
Common Temperament Behaviors When Stressed

	Common Behaviors When Stressed
Temperament 1	• Takes things personally
	• Becomes more concerned about acceptance of self than tangible results
	• Acts impulsively—heart exclusively over mind
	• Overreacts
	• Becomes inattentive to detail
	• Is emotionally unstable
Temperament 2	• Exhibits extreme aloofness and withdrawal
	• Hesitates to act without precedent
	• Yields position to avoid controversy
	• Refuses to communicates (the silent treatment)
	• Communicates through sarcasm
	• Becomes perfectionistic (usually due to severe performance anxiety
	• Is highly critical of self and others
	• Becomes indecisive, refusing to act without more and more and more data
Temperament 3	• Tries to control situations and others
	• Relies exclusively on rules and regulations (closed to new ideas)
	• Is anxious and worried
	• Insists on maintaining status quo
	• Resists starting on new, unstructured assignments
	• Refuses to change
	• Holds onto past experiences and feelings
	• Waits for orders before acting
	• Experiences psychosomatic problems
Temperament 4	• Oversteps prerogatives and group norms (may become defiant)
	• Stimulates anxiety in others
	• Dominates others
	• Is restless
	• Becomes blunt and sarcastic
	• Sulks when not in limelight
	• Is critical and fault-finding
	• Resists participation in groups
	• Interrupts and/or ignores others

Most of us have participated in work groups, but few of us have stopped to consider what made it a "work group." Probably the work group was well coordinated; everyone had a role to play and there was an understanding of and commitment to a common goal. Typically, four key elements differentiate work groups from other types of groups:[3]

1. The group has a charter or reason for working together.
2. Members of the group are interdependent—they need and share each other's experience, ability, and dedication to arrive at mutual goals.
3. Group members believe that working together as a group leads to more effective decisions than working in isolation.
4. The group is accountable as a functioning unit usually within a larger organizational context.

Determining the Context of Work Groups

When facilitating a group for the first time, it is vital to examine the context within which the group will be formed and operated. Even new groups have "history" that will undoubtedly affect their performance, and facilitators need to explore this history. The exercise below provides a list of questions applicable to facilitators who are either forming new groups or are assuming the facilitation of a previously formed group. Answering these questions can assist the facilitator in better understanding group behaviors and selecting appropriate interaction strategies.

GROUP CONTEXT QUESTIONS

Questions to ask when forming a new group:

- Why is the group being formed?
- What criteria will be used for determining group membership?
- Have those designated to serve on this work group had previous experiences on work groups? If so, have those experiences been successful? If not, what problems might you anticipate?
- Will the culture of the group reflect the larger organizational culture? If not, how will these differences affect the work-group operation?
- How will the group be organized?
- How will the group develop its charge (overall task/assignment to be completed) and charter (group purpose, goals, roles, and procedures)?
- What are the potential member's views about work groups? About facilitators?

Questions to ask when assuming the facilitation of an existing group:

- Why was the group formed? When was the group formed? How was group membership determined?
- Do clearly delineated goals and objectives exist? If yes, how were they determined? Are the goals and objectives still appropriate to the larger organizational mission?
- To whom is the group accountable? How is this accountability practiced?
- How has the group determined leadership? Does the group have an organizational chart?
- Has group membership remained consistent? If yes, are the reasons for consistent membership reasonable and valid? If not, how and why has membership changed?
- What are some of the groups' successes? What are some of their failures/challenges?
- Has the group worked with a facilitator previously? If so, what were their experiences?
- How is the group viewed by the larger organization? Does the group have institutional support? If no, why not? If yes, what does the support entail?
- How have plans and individual assignments been developed?
- Is the group's culture similar or different from that of the organization? If different, how is the group affected?

Working through the Stages of Groups

As groups are formed and become operational, those that are successful typically negotiate four stages. Identified initially by Bruce Tuckman in the 1960s, the stages are familiarly known as Forming/Initial Norming, Storming, Renorming, and Performing. Ideally, the facilitator will begin with the group as it is forming, and can thus assist the group in addressing the four stages from the onset. In those instances when facilitators are introduced after the group has been established, it is important that they identify the stage the group is experiencing as soon as possible. Next, the facilitator should educate the group about the stages of group development, help them identify what stage they are currently are in, and guide them through the successful completion of each stage. It is important to note that every group must work through each stage in order to reach working stability and achieve optimal performance. Tables 2.6 through 2.9 explain the four stages and their associated tasks and behaviors and provide guidelines and questions for facilitators to both identify and work through each stage.

Table 2.6
Stage 1—Forming/Initial Norming

Tasks to accomplish	• Achieve an understanding of the purpose and charge of the group
	• Learn about the other group members
	• Establish initial group interaction protocol
Ways to accomplish tasks	• Clarify the purpose of and charge to the group
	• Introduce group members
	• Assess the resources of each group member
	• Initiate activities that help identify the working styles, skills, knowledge, and experiences of group members
	• Implement interaction protocol
Observable characteristics of group members in Forming/Initial Norming Stage	• Uncertainty about group's purpose and goals
	• Enthusiasm
	• Tentativeness
	• Feelings of anxiety
	• Seeking a sense of belonging and group identity
	• Awkwardness
Questions to be answered	• Why are we here?
	• What are we expected to accomplish?
	• Who am I working with?
	• How will we work together?
Residual problems if group does not successfully complete Forming/Initial Norming Stage	• Group members with different ideas of where the group is headed and how to get there
	• Lack of clarity in group's charge and purpose
	• Unidentified group-member, capital, and administrative resources

Based on information from Richard 6G. Weaver and John D. Farrell, *Managers as Facilitators* (San Francisco: Berrett-Koehler Publishers, Inc., 1997), p. 68.

When groups experience changes in membership, their charge, or their facilitators, they will need to once again go through the four stages. Furthermore, groups may appear to have successfully completed a stage when in fact they have not fully understood or embraced it. Facilitators need to identify this situation as quickly as possible and guide the group back through that stage and all subsequent stages to ensure effective group functioning.

In Stage 1—Forming/Initial Norming—the facilitator begins by helping the group clarify the reasons it was formed (purpose) and what it is responsible for accomplishing (charge). Additionally, the group establishes its expectations of its members, as well as methods of accountability and guidelines or rules for interacting (for example, meeting protocols and group behaviors).

Stage 2—Storming—is a "natural" byproduct of groups learning how to work together and can be viewed as a sign that group members feel comfortable enough with each other to move beyond the more superficial level of interactions found in Stage 1. As the group members begin working on their respective assignments, confusion occurs. Misunderstood or unclear expectations emerge; members can feel anxious, fearful, frustrated, and angry. Original plans, norms, and procedures prove faulty or limited, leaving members without direction or adequate resources or expertise to complete their activities. In other words, a whole host of issues can arise as a result of unanticipated outcomes. Facilitation at this point means introducing constructive methods of addressing conflict and resolving problems.

As part of addressing these group conflicts, Stage 3—Renorming—begins. During this stage, group members revise the procedures, guidelines, and protocol that have proven limited or unsatisfactory. Open communication is reinstituted, group purposes and goals are clarified as needed, and trust in each other and the group process is restored.

Table 2.7
Stage 2—Storming

Tasks to accomplish	• Identify what group members expect from each other • Identify how group members expect to work together
Ways to accomplish tasks	• Openly express expectations of individual members • Identify member differences • Experience constructive conflict
Observable characteristics of group members in Storming Stage	• Conflict, both within and outside of group • Ambiguity in member roles • Strong resistance to group formation • Frustration • Discrepancy between hopes and reality • Competition among members • Formation of cliques
Questions to be answered	• What do I expect from others? • What do others expect from me? • What do I think and feel about these expectations?
Residual problems if group does not successfully complete Storming Stage	• Group members upset with the group because their expectations are not being met • Group members feeling they are doing most of the group work • Group members feeling they are not important or useful to the group

Based on information from Weaver and Farrell, p. 69.

Table 2.8
Stage 3—Renorming

Tasks to accomplish	• Resolve differences in what group members expect of each other • Review how they will work together
Ways to accomplish tasks	• Reestablish group rules to include areas not addressed originally • Revisit the group's charge and charter • Reexamine how the group will interact and perform with one another (make modifications as necessary)
Observable characteristics of group members in Renorming Stage	• Negotiation among group members • Beginning to work together more smoothly as group • Members supporting leadership and one another • Group oriented to accomplishing mutual goals • Developing harmony, trust, and respect within and outside of group • Using constructive problem solving and conflict resolution • Esprit de corps
Question to be answered	• How are we going to work together in ways that are mutually satisfying?
Residual problems if group does not successfully complete Renorming Stage	• Group members not in agreement on how to work together • Group members working at cross-purposes with one another

Based on information from Weaver and Farrell, p. 70.

Performing—Stage 4—is the true productive stage of the group. Group members assign and accomplish tasks smoothly, communicate effectively, encourage collaboration, perform to mutually determined quality standards, and use conflict as an opportunity to grow. Group members are interdependent, experiencing high levels of satisfaction in their individual and collective contributions.

Establishing the Group Charge and Charter

Establishing group clarity is essential to the group accomplishing its designated assignments. Clarity can be achieved by defining the group's charge and charter as early in the group process as possible (during Stage 1, Forming/Initial Norming is most advantageous).

Table 2.9
Stage 4—Performing

Task to accomplish	• Produce the output expected of the group
Ways to accomplish tasks	• Assign tasks that will lead group to accomplish its charge • Continually clarify roles of each group member • Encourage collaboration with other group members • Establish quality levels of outcomes • Address problems and issues as they arise
Observable characteristics of group members in Performing Stage	• Interdependence of group members • Achieving consistent, excellent performance • High level of group-member satisfaction
Question to be answered	• How will we know when we have been successful?
Residual problems if group does not successfully complete Performing Stage	• Work not getting accomplished • Group unable to determine when performance is substandard • Group unable to celebrate accomplishments • Ongoing dissatisfaction with group • Ongoing dissatisfaction with individual role within group

Based on information from Weaver and Farrell, p. 71.

The group's charge is its overall assignment, the achievement of the tasks for which it has been formed. Its charter is the delineation of how it will function and includes its purpose, goals, roles, and procedures. Purposes typically outline why the group was formed, how it fits into the overall organization, and its benefits to the organization. Goals are statements that speak to how the group will fulfill its purpose. The roles define individual group member responsibilities, and when coupled with the goals substantiate and justify the purpose. Finally, the procedures depict how the group will interact both socially and technically, including such things as meeting protocols, responsibility for procuring resources, and timelines for task completion.

Identifying the Work Group's Charge. Usually identifying the group's charge is a fairly straightforward process, as most groups are formed to complete a specific assignment, or charge. It is imperative, however, that the facilitator promote discussion about the charge among the group members so that questions can be generated and answered and individual ownership of the charge can begin. Regardless of the time it takes to fashion and adopt the charge, facilitators are strongly urged to spend all the time necessary to satisfy the group. Without the resultant ownership that comes from the group embracing the charge, group members have little reason to believe or participate in the group process.

The charge should be stated as specifically and concisely as possible to provide unwavering focus throughout the group's task. It should also reflect the overall organizational mission and strategic plan. The following are some examples of charges with a high degree of clarity:

- The finance team will have a five-year projected growth plan, outlining an annual increase in sales of 5 percent by June 30 to present to the administrative team for review.
- By September 1, the human resources team will present to the board of directors an employee training plan for introducing the new salary structure and performance review to all organizational employees.

Once the group's charge has been established and accepted by the group, it should be shared with the larger organization. The reasoning is multifold:

- Groups typically operate within a larger organization. Keeping the full organization apprised of group activities and progress can eliminate misconceptions, enlist wide-based support, and encourage nongroup employees to identify resources needed by the group.
- When the overall organization is informed of group activities on an ongoing basis, it is in a better position to understand how group efforts sustain the organizational strategy. Employees are reminded consistently of what the organization is trying to accomplish and of their roles in its success.
- Larger organizations often run the risk of duplicating efforts. When all employees are educated about individual work-group activities, duplicative efforts can be more readily identified and addressed.

Developing the Work Group's Charter. The group's charter is developed immediately after its charge is clarified and accepted by all group members. As with the charge, the facilitator should work with the full work group to create the charter.

Expanding and clarifying the group charge even further, the charter has four components:[4]

1. *Purpose* explains why the group exists, how it relates to the overall organizational strategy, to whom it is responsible, and how it will benefit the organization.

2. *Goals* provide details about what the group will do, how it will accomplish its responsibilities, who will assume responsibility for what, and when the activities will be completed.

3. *Roles* delineate what each group member will be responsible for accomplishing; roles are usually based on members' respective expertise and experience.

4. *Procedures* define how the group plans to work together both within and outside the group; interaction (social) and activity (technical) procedures assist groups in relating and sharing information appropriately and expeditiously.

Since the charter follows directly from the charge, facilitators should begin working with the group on crafting its charter as soon as the charge has been adopted. Furthermore, the four charter components—purpose, goals, roles, and procedures—should be addressed in sequence. Figure 2.1 outlines the charge and charter development.

Coordinating Chart and Charter Creation with the Group Development Stages

Earlier in this chapter, we introduced the four stages of group development—Forming/Initial Norming, Storming, Renorming, and Performing—and provided details about the primary tasks to be accomplished in each stage (refer to Tables 2.6 through 2.9). These four stages dovetail easily with the tasks associated with creating the group's charge and charter. Figure 2.2 suggests those charge and charter components to be completed and applied throughout the four group development stages. As an example, the charge is introduced for discussion, finalization, and adoption by the work group during Stage 1—Forming/Initial Norming—which encourages clarification of the group's chief function. Initial work on the group's purpose as well as group interaction protocols are completed during this stage as well. Once the charge and purpose are adopted, they serve as the primary focus of all subsequent work-group efforts occurring throughout the remainder of the development stages.

When the facilitator ensures that the group's charge and charter are clearly delineated and have been understood, supported, and adopted by every work-group member, the group will have successfully negotiated the four group development stages and is positioned for peak performance. Members are clear about organizational expectations for the group, focused on the overall task, engaged in their respective activities, and ready to willingly share their expertise with other group members.

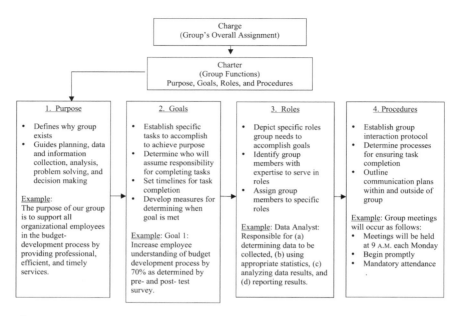

Figure 2.1 Group Charge and Charter Development Components

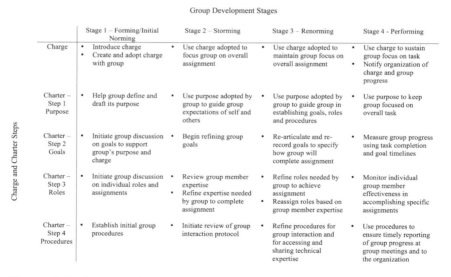

Figure 2.2 Creating the Charge and Charter within the Four Group Developmental Stages

As with all facets of life, work groups are dynamic, particularly as they usually work within larger organizational contexts that dictate their continuation. Myriad external and internal unforeseen circumstances can compromise their assignments; institutional and/or customer support for their efforts might waver as strategic priorities vacillate or group membership changes. In other words, a whole host of issues can arise, causing upheaval within even the most vigilantly facilitated groups. It is up to the facilitator to help groups move through such issues by identifying and resolving problems and to ultimately restore each member's commitment to exemplary, self-gratifying performance.

To maximize the potential of work groups created by using the facilitative techniques proposed in this chapter, the remaining chapters include tools and techniques for facilitators to both maintain the evolution of groups that are progressing as planned and to intervene to bring groups that have gone awry back on target. Resolving conflicts that will inevitably occur, inspiring and motivating group members experiencing setbacks, working with cultural and individual diversity, and instituting productive and meaningful work sessions are all real and probable concerns for facilitators.

In spirit, effective facilitation works with an intriguing human color palette. Challenged with creating groups from blank canvases, facilitators envision their completed pictures and begin integrating the diverse colors, patterns, and shapes at their disposal into a pleasing, harmonious whole. When creating, facilitators intuit those colors and patterns that blend, while boldly combining those that threaten riotous cacophony. In the end, the picture's beauty is in its synchronization of style, ingenuity, differences, unforeseen opportunities, and commitment.

CHAPTER IMPLICATIONS

- Self-awareness is fundamental to a facilitator's success. Managers assuming facilitative roles need to understand their interaction preferences to determine how they will influence the group.
- Every individual has a preferred learning, working, and living style or styles. No one style is better or worse than another; however, certain styles are better in some situations than others. Facilitators need to be able to elicit those style behaviors that serve the group best.
- Groups produce the best results when they are composed of members with different styles. Style differences, however, can initially create inherent tensions among group members; facilitators must guide group members beyond this tension and encourage appreciation of different perspectives.

- Groups have four developmental stages—Forming/Initial Norming, Storming, Renorming, and Performing—that must be negotiated in sequence for optimal group achievement. It is up to the facilitator to identify these stages and recognize when the group has successfully completed each stage.
- Groups need a clear charge and charter to attain their assigned tasks. At the group's onset, facilitators should direct the group through each charge and charter step to maximize individual member ownership of and clarity about the group process.

QUESTIONS FOR REFLECTION

1. To what extent have I identified and defined my values, beliefs, needs, and attitudes about facilitation? How well will my facilitation values, beliefs, needs, and attitudes serve me in my facilitation efforts? Serve the groups with which I work or will work?
2. What temperament theory instruments am I interested in investigating? In using?
3. Do I have the expertise necessary to use a temperament theory instrument with the work groups I facilitate? If not, am I able to find and utilize expertise?
4. How well do I understand the four stages—Forming/Initial Norming, Storming, Renorming, and Performing—of group development? What is my level of comfort with guiding work groups successfully through each step? What additional education do I need about facilitating groups through the four stages?
5. How comfortable am I in facilitating the work group's creation of a charge and charter? What additional skills do I need to facilitate each charge and charter component? How can I attain these skills?

THREE

Facilitating Inspirational Environments

The workplace can be a productive, constructive, meaningful part of life. In fact, given the decline of many of our social institutions such as family, church and local government, the workplace may be the best place, and may be the only place, to realize goals interdependently, working side by side with people of different backgrounds, education levels, races, countries of origin and organizational responsibilities.[1]

In Chapter 2, we presented information on facilitating work groups; that is, how to facilitate the creation of a work group by (a) encouraging facilitator and group member self-awareness, (b) identifying group member individual strengths and challenges in group settings, (c) moving the group through the four-step group development process, and (d) creating the group's charge and charter. We also referred to work groups as dynamic, complex, evolving social systems that adapt to their environments. Thus it follows that once a work group has been established, the environment in which it operates becomes crucial to its ongoing success.

In this chapter, we explain how managers can maximize not only work-group success but also the success of all the employees for whom they bear responsibility by facilitating an inspiring working atmosphere—an

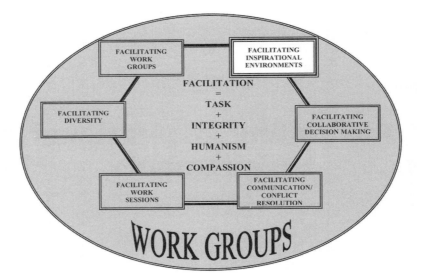

In this chapter, you will learn to:

- Engage employees in their work

- Operate within employees' expectations of the workplace

- Motivate your employees to higher productivity

- Assess motivational levels in your employees

- Identify and measure an inspirational workplace

atmosphere wherein workers are engaged, motivated, perform at their peak, and derive a high degree of satisfaction from their responsibilities.

VALUING WORK

Most employees seek satisfaction in their work, hoping to attain a measure of self-fulfillment. Although the reasons they acquire employment may appear as chiefly fiscal (even to themselves), the reality is that people typically define themselves by what they do and how well they perform the attendant activities. A substantial part of their lives is spent working, and their workplace experiences have a significant impact on their overall sense of well-being.

To encourage employee satisfaction, managers need to genuinely embrace and promote the enjoyment of work as a core value. All employees should have the opportunity to perform at their peak, stretching their skills and expanding their personal and professional capabilities. Managers want to capitalize on the fact that the majority of their employees desire to grow in their work, and that assigning boring, routine, meaningless tasks strangles their creativity and interest.

Engaging Employees

Truly engaged employees are those who add value to the overall organization by operating at peak performance and sustaining productivity levels that promote profits. To a large extent, managers influence employee engagement by ensuring that they establish an environment in which their employees can flourish.

Managers as effective facilitators need to model the behaviors they desire in their employees. First and foremost, they must be engaged themselves if they expect their employees to be engaged, just as they need to practice respect, trust, and commitment to cultivate the same within their workers. Employees sense when managers are insincere and react by disassociating from the workplace. Hence, managers must be prepared to not only spend the time necessary to enlist employee engagement, but also must genuinely care that their employees become engaged.

Goals, Rules, and Control.   Encouraging employee engagement means that managers/facilitators make certain that every employee has concrete goals, manageable rules, and a sense of potential control. All employees want to be a part of the greater organizational good, to know that they are making meaningful contributions and that what they are doing matters in socially relevant ways. Operating as facilitators, managers can utilize a number of tactics to encourage employees in this direction:

- Give employees the latitude necessary to see their specific activities through to their ends.
- Show them how their activities are part of the larger picture.
- Understand that their individual activities must lead to conclusions or outcomes that are meaningful to them.
- Ensure that the steps for completing activities are manageable and that all necessary resources are available.
- Allow them to determine the specific methods they will use to accomplish the activities.
- Use the power of positive expectations—believing and exuding confidence in their ability to succeed.
- Encourage celebrations of accomplishments.

Decisive Action and Challenges. All employees must have opportunities to act decisively and match their abilities to the challenges at hand, and managers/facilitators can encourage decisive actions by doing the following:

- Ensure that employees are actively involved in the situations surrounding their work responsibilities, especially that they have a central role in determining the outcomes they are expected to perform.
- Foster their growth by encouraging them to make more challenging choices, while at the same time easing anxiety and fear of negative consequences if they fail.
- Involve people in the planning of their total operation, encouraging their full understanding of their and others' roles.

Concentration. Employees must have environments free from distractions to allow them time for concentration. Workers need to give the necessary attention, sensitivity, and awareness to their efforts. When they are able to do this, their outcomes take on higher importance; worries, concerns and distractions are gone. Managers/facilitators can sponsor concentration by paying attention to the following:

- Provide a work space that is conducive to concentration, meaning free of incessant interruptions (for example, constantly ringing phones, ongoing interruptions from colleagues), where thinking and planning can be done with continuity.
- Understand where employees' knowledge and experience fall short of what is needed and helping them gain what they need without taking away their initiative. Workers need to know they have their manager's ongoing support as they strive to complete their assignments.

Timely Feedback. All employees need timely feedback. As they are working, employees have to know whether or not to continue in the same vein or change direction. Relying on annual or even semi-annual reviews is insufficient; employees learn best when the experience is still fresh. There are some important considerations to remember when providing feedback:

- Understand that workers have individual preferences on how and when to receive feedback and act accordingly.
- Work with employees to help them measure and evaluate their own efforts by asking questions such as the following:

  - How do you think your work is measuring up to the proposed outcomes?
  - What do you think you're doing well? Less well?
  - What do you think would improve your performance? Do you need additional resources? Training? Other types of assistance?

In our experiences as managers, facilitators, and consultants, we have found that employees reporting a high degree of satisfaction in their work and whose managers regard as highly engaged need concrete goals, manageable rules, and a sense of potential control; opportunities to act decisively and match their abilities to the challenges at hand; time for and work space conducive to concentration; and timely feedback.

Essentially, facilitating engaged employees requires that managers know each of their employees well so that interactions can be relevant and meaningful and they can achieve mutual understanding. Assuming that as managers you have taken advantage of temperament assessment strategies, specific methods for personalizing interactions with your employees are included in Table 3.1. These methods, identified through research and practical experience, have proven useful in establishing rapport with both subordinates and colleagues. We encourage you to employ these behaviors when working with the different temperaments.

Understanding Employee Expectations of Workplaces

We introduced in Chapter 1 some of the changes that are occurring in U.S. workplaces. Organizations have learned that highly structured chains of command operating in relative isolation don't lend themselves to making sound decisions in today's complex, quick-acting business environments. Employees play increasingly crucial roles in honing their organizations' competitive edge.

Table 3.1
Facilitator Strategies for Creating Inspiring Workplaces

	Temperament 1	Temperament 2	Temperament 3	Temperament 4
Employees RESPOND BEST TO	• Idealism • Insight • People-centeredness • Warm personality • Inclusiveness • Communi-cation • Motivation • Harmony • Respect • Sincerity	• Vision • Analysis • Autonomy • Independence • Theory • "Big picture" • Intellect • Strategy • Logic • Challenge • Resources	• Truthfulness • Reliability • Clarity • Organization • Fairness • Punctuality • Realism • Respect for tradition and status quo • Thoroughness	• Stimulation • Directness • Initiative • Action • Artistry • Creativity • Pragmatism • Flexibility • Risk taking • Excitement
When facilitating ESTABLISH	• A trusting, friendly, harmonious environment • Opportunities for personal growth • A vision they can believe in • Rapport	• Global outcomes • Challenging, stretching goals that are difficult to reach • An autonomous environment • Evaluation criteria • Models and systems	• Precise expectations and procedures • Definite lines of authority • Firm deadlines • A reliable, predictable and consistent environment • Clear commu-nication channels	• Risk-taking rewards • Variety of tasks and responsibili-ties • Freedom and independence • A flexible, self-paced, fun environment • Face-to-face dialogue
When facilitating BE	• Inclusive • Inspiring and positive • Open and receptive to input • People-centered	• Competent • Challenging and strategic • Knowledge-able • Convincing • Open to change	• Decisive • Well organized • Hard working • Direct and fair	• Responsive • Open-ended and flexible • Stimulating • Direct and honest
When facilitating USE	• Acknowledge-ment of unique contributions • Personal proach • Praise and encouragement for efforts • Care with human interactions	• Minimal guidelines • Minimal directives • Logic • Analysis	• Encourage-ment when needed • Discretion in appreciation • Your own hard work to motivate	• Your ability to "fly by the seat of the pants" • Rewards for initiative and daring • Action • Humor

For their part, employees have come to expect certain workplace rights and privileges that traditionally were not customary. Managers must realize what workers expect to exist in the workplace as they implement strategies to facilitate peak performance levels. Failure to do so can seriously hamper even the most tried-and-true methods of inspiring employees. Following is a distillation of workplace characteristics influencing employees' behaviors and expectations:[2]

- *Representation.* Today, employees at all organizational levels are represented in board rooms. They are accustomed to participating in central decision making and influencing corporate policy and procedures.
- *Autonomous work groups.* More and more frequently, employees are organized in small self-managing, peer-supervision groups. They are responsible for organizing their own work and ensuring quality control.
- *Co-ownership and co-management.* Historical distinctions among owners, managers, and workers have blurred. Employees are often co-owners with other shareholders; they have a vested interest in the organization's goals and outcomes and freely share their opinions. Increasingly, management is diversified; staff members regardless of organizational level have greater autonomy in decision making and more overall responsibility.
- *Consent cultures.* Today's organizations inform, confer with, and consult their staff rather than control them. Employees are used to being kept abreast of corporate plans and asked for their support in achieving outcomes.
- *Flexible management.* Managers are expected to move fluidly from making decisions *for* people to making decisions *with* people and delegating decision making *to* people. Leadership changes depending on the project at hand and the expertise needed; positional authority is seldom exercised to exert power over employees.
- *Project work groups.* Management has shifted from hierarchical command to authority that resides within work groups composed of specialists. Usually the groups are horizontally structured, members work interdependently, and groups might last only as long as the required tasks.
- *Learning organizations.* Organizations view themselves as learning systems, in which human resource development is continuously used to make them self-transforming and self-actualizing. Employees are encouraged to be open to new challenges and assume ever-greater responsibility.
- *Shift from wages to contracting and networking.* Organizations are paying people fees for work done independently to certain standards, rather than paying wages for time spent under managerial control. Organizations frequently contract out work to a network of professionals, including

individuals and teams. "Employees" operate outside the formal work-place, exercising a high degree of independence.

- *Centralized administration.* Large organizations have shifted to central-ized oversight of a network of many small, semiautonomous enter-prises. Employees are used to having a unique role in these smaller, more "humanized" offices.

In summary, encouraged to think creatively and respond quickly to developing situations, employees exercise a considerable amount of self-rule and self-determination in today's workplaces. Organizations depend on their employees for productivity, increasing corporate profits, and shaping competitive efforts. Managing employees under these circumstances means acknowledging and respecting every worker's heightened professionalism and contribution.

Motivating Yourself and Others

When managers consider the "hows" and "whys" of motivating their employees, it's best to begin with how they themselves are motivated to achieve. Once they understand their own motivating factors, they can more effectively stimulate others. To orient your managerial thinking, take some time to respond to the following exercise.

Think about a recent situation at work when you were highly motivated and productive. Write a short description of this situation and then explain why you felt so motivated and productive. Which of these "reasons" were under your personal, direct control?

In the situation you've described, your high level of motivation and productivity was most likely a consequence of a large number of factors. The key portion of this exercise, however, is identifying those factors under your direct and personal control; they reflect the chief sources of personal motivation and productivity. It's important to sort out those factors that are a function of your personal motivation needs and work habits (that is, those factors under your control) and those that are a result of external factors (for example, organizational policies and procedures, resource constraints, or managerial differences).

Identifying those factors that are not under your control and that im-pede your motivation helps ameliorate frustration. Furthermore, once you're able to separate motivational factors into those two categories, you're in a stronger position to help subordinates do the same. Ironically, the more one recognizes those factors that are not under one's control, the greater the level of perceived control and the lower the level of frustration.[3]

Factors Contributing to Motivation

Employee commitment to the organization, to the task at hand, and to personal success is vital to sustaining motivation. Commitment is fostered most strongly by involving employees in decisions that affect them. Managers can facilitate commitment by consistently enjoining participative decision making and mutually determined outcome quality standards. Commitment also fosters employees who value internal goals and intrinsic rewards and who care a great deal about the tasks they perform. Perhaps most importantly, a high level of commitment protects employees from the adverse effects of stress.

Employees become more motivated when they are challenged. Their interest is piqued when given the opportunity to meet an appropriate level of challenge. When they are encouraged to search continuously for reasonable risks and opportunities to pursue "stretch goals," employees will uphold a high degree of motivation.

Understanding and adopting a clear vision or purpose is a key factor in motivation. Both managers and their employees must believe in the organization's vision. And the activities they are asked to accomplish and the methods used to accomplish them must be congruent with their internal values or buy-in and ownership may be thwarted.

Motivated workers require equilibrium between acting autonomously and responding to clear and specific goals. They need enough discretion to exercise their judgment, but cannot be left without guidance or standards. Motivated employees "feel" they have the control they need over the conditions necessary to complete their tasks.

When performing, motivated employees experience transcendence; that is, they surpass previous performance levels. They set higher and higher achievement standards and seek ways to continuously improve. They are driven to excel at whatever they attempt.

Motivation is also a matter of balance. Employees who experience joy and pleasure in work, home, family, friends, and play typically exhibit high motivation in the workplace. Additionally, all of these aspects work in concert to generate enthusiasm across all life aspects.

Recognizing Motivated Employees

Highly motivated (and thus highly productive) individuals usually share the following attributes:

- They are results-oriented because of a sense of personal mission.
- They are able to display the dual capacities of self-management and team mastery.
- They are capable of making corrections and managing change.[4]

Motivation typically wanes when employees' needs go unsatisfied. Sometimes the reasons for employee dissatisfaction are beyond the manager's control (for example, a depressed economy or the loss of key customers). However, as we mentioned earlier in this chapter, more often than not managers are able to facilitate higher motivation levels. Managers observing decreased motivation in their employees can use the following assessment to help diagnose the underlying causes. The assessment offers a grouping of common employee needs that when left unmet can lead to discouragement, frustration, and confusion.

ASSESSING MOTIVATION FACTORS

This assessment is designed to help managers diagnose potential underlying problems in employees experiencing little or diminishing motivation. In the first column, rate how important you believe the grouping of needs are to your employees. In the second column, rate the extent to which you have addressed these needs.

With some modifications to wording, this same instrument can be completed by your employees. Ask them to rate the importance to them of the grouping of needs, and then the extent to which the needs have been met by the organization.

VERY LOW	1	2	3	4	5	VERY HIGH

Importance	Opportunity	
_____	_____	1. Direction, purpose, role clarity
_____	_____	2. Belonging, group membership, affiliation
_____	_____	3. Compensation, recognition, rewards
_____	_____	4. Productivity, impact, achievement
_____	_____	5. Outcomes, evaluations, standards
_____	_____	6. Sensitivity, consideration, support
_____	_____	7. Challenge, variety, stimulation
_____	_____	8. Coordination, predictability, control
_____	_____	9. Resources, cooperation, expertise
_____	_____	10. Celebration, satisfaction, growth

Clarifying the Managerial Mindset

Achieving clarity about their management responsibilities is paramount for managers facilitating inspirational working climates. Clarity in their roles means that managers are able to balance authoritative guidance

Table 3.2
Managerial Dimensions

Dimension	Description	Question/s to be Addressed
Operating	The overall planning of the project that includes • Identifying resources • Methods for implementing activities • Supervising work in the field • Structuring workplace activities • Establishing outcome benchmarks • Setting timelines	• How can the work in progress be supervised and managed?
Planning	The "power as authority" aspect that includes • Making decisions about the project objectives • Deciding the work goals of employees and work groups • Implementing the protocol for actualizing the goals	• How can decisions about the objectives and work plans for the employees/work group be made?
Confronting	The conflict-resolution and problem-solving aspect that includes • Raising employees' and/or work-group members' consciousness about nonproductive behaviors that are interfering with job satisfaction and work effectiveness	• How can the employees' and/or work-group members' consciousness be raised about these matters?
Meaning	This includes five interrelated aspects about the meaning of work • Knowledge required to perform the tasks • Learning acquired while performing the tasks	• How will each of these aspects be given to and found in the tasks the employees and/or work-group members will be performing?

Table 3.2 Continued

Dimension	Description	Question/s to be Addressed
	• Knowledge of the effects of doing the tasks • Nature of the work is congruent with employee values • Work has moral and social significance to world	
Valuing	This is the intuitive, moral aspect that includes • Creating a work culture with core values and respect for one another • Encouraging employees to be genuine, open, and honest • Honoring the inherent dignity of every employee • Acting with integrity	• How can a work culture with core values and a climate of respect and integrity be created?
Feeling	This reflects the affective aspect that includes • Managing the fulfillment of human needs and interests in and through work • Dealing with emotions and interpersonal relationships • Attending to empathy, participation, collaboration, and rapport of all employees	• How will job satisfaction, emotions, relationships, and significance among employees and/or work-group members be handled?

Robert E. Quinn, Sue R. Faerman, Michael P. Thompson, and Michael R. McGrath, *Becoming a Master Manager: A Competency Framework* (New York: John Wiley & Sons, 1990), pp. 350–51.

with employee autonomy, match challenge with abilities, and help set realistic expectations for performance and outcomes.

In Table 3.2, we introduce an overview of six primary managerial dimensions, include a brief definition of each dimension, and provide questions managers need to answer prior to launching projects with work groups and/or individual employees. Spending time contemplating these questions up front can save costly "wheel spinning" as well as employee and managerial bewilderment as projects unfold.

These dimensions interweave and overlap and are mutually supportive of each other. They are all needed, together in conscious use, for effective facilitation of an inspirational environment. The successful facilitator is one who can flexibly shift among them.

Measuring an Inspired Workplace

How can managers tell when they have successfully facilitated a healthy, inspiring workplace? Typically, their employees freely exhibit many common behaviors across multiple situations. They visibly show the following characteristics:

- *Interdependence.* They trust one another and look to each other as resources that can be counted on. They make decisions freely and respect others' decisions. They work together to achieve the best possible results. They provide inspiration to one another.
- *Trustworthiness and respect.* They maintain confidentiality. They are supportive of one another and their comments are positive and constructive. They operate within the boundaries of workplace norms (for example, they attend meetings regularly and promptly).
- *Open, honest communication.* They encourage one another to express ideas fully. They listen well, express their emotions, and speak openly about their feelings. Their decisions reflect emotional as well as practical concerns.
- *Responsibility and accountability for group decisions.* They suspend personal agendas and "glory." They support outcomes regardless of success or failure and are committed to the success of all project activities. They assume leadership as necessary.
- *Viewing criticism and conflict as opportunities to learn.* They encourage diverse perspectives and avoid defensiveness when others disagree with their ideas. They work to ensure that all viewpoints are explored.
- *Fun.* They celebrate individual and group accomplishments and take pride in the achievements of one another.

WORKPLACE CLIMATE ASSESSMENT

1. Goals and Objectives

1	2	3	4	5	6	7

There is a lack of commonly understood goals and objectives.

Work-group members/ employees understand and agree on goals and objectives.

2. Use of Group-Member/Employee Strengths

1	2	3	4	5	6	7

Group members/employees' abilities are not fully recognized/used.

Group-members/employees' abilities are fully recognized and used.

3. Trust and Conflict Resolution

1	2	3	4	5	6	7

Little trust among group members/employees is evident.

A high degree of trust exists among group members/ employees and conflict is dealt with openly and effectively.

4. Leadership

1	2	3	4	5	6	7

One person dominates and leadership roles are not carried out or shared.

There is full participation in leadership; leadership roles are shared by group members/employees.

5. Protocol and Procedures

1	2	3	4	5	6	7

There is little protocol evident and no procedures guide group members/employees.

Effective protocol and procedures exist to guide group/employees; all support these procedures.

6. Interpersonal Communications

1	2	3	4	5	6	7

Communications among group members/employees are closed and guarded.

Communications among group members/employees are open and participative.

7. Problem Solving/Decision Making

1	2	3	4	5	6	7

Group members/employees have no agreed-upon approaches for problem solving and decision making.

Groups members/employees have well-established and agreed-upon approaches to problem solving and decision making.

8. Risk Taking and Creativity

1	2	3	4	5	6	7

Group members/employees are rigid, avoid taking risks and do not question how/ why things are done.

Group members/ employees experiment with different, creative approaches and solutions.

9. Evaluation/Feedback

1	2	3	4	5	6	7

Group members/ employees never evaluate or receive feedback on their functioning or progress.

Group members/ employees often evaluate give and receive feedback on their functioning and progress.

10. Organizational Ownership

1	2	3	4	5	6	7

Group members/employees never receive updates about or have input on overall organizational plans.

Group members/ employees regularly receive updates about and opportunities for input on organizational plans.

11. Organizational Support

1	2	3	4	5	6	7

Group members/employees receive no support or acknowledgement from the larger organization for their contributions.

Group members/ employees receive ongoing support and acknowledgement from the larger organization for their contributions.

12. Adequacy of Resources

1	2	3	4	5	6	7

Group members/ employees frequently experience a shortage of resources necessary to complete their responsibilities.

Group members/ employees always have the resources necessary to complete their responsibilities.

13. Celebration

1	2	3	4	5	6	7

Group members/employees spend no time celebrating their accomplishments.

Celebrating accomplishments is a high group-member/employee priority.

We also include an assessment—"Workplace Climate Assessment"— for measuring workplace climate more concretely. The assessment instrument addresses the chief factors underlying inspirational cultures that are presented in this chapter. Assessment results can be used to pinpoint and thus improve weaker areas. This assessment is designed for use by both managers/facilitators and employees. Comparing the results can illuminate miscommunication and perceptual differences obstructing rapport among managers and employees.

SUMMARY

Facilitating inspiring environments requires multiple strategies, the majority of which fall to the manager for implementing or initiating. Managers first must understand their own inspirational level—to inspire one must be inspired—and what inspires them. Clarity in their roles and how they interface with their corporate culture is imperative.

Facilitating inspiring workplaces also means focusing on employees— what gives them satisfaction? How are they motivated? What can I do to make their workplace meaningful to them? Managers become not only planners, resource gatherers, and supervisors, but also cheerleaders and coaches. Certainly they are responsible for getting the job done, but not at the sacrifice of employee well-being. In short, managers must take great care of the organization's most important resource—the employees.

To recap chapter highlights, we list some of the strategies that managers can use to inspire employees:

- Show authentic appreciation and recognition of current and future employee contributions.
- Incorporate employee ideas into significant business practices.
- Give timely, frank, and constructive evaluations of present performance.
- Provide support during major changes, including a reasonable transition time when termination is anticipated.
- Frequently communicate accurate information about the organization's vision, goals, and progress.
- Illustrate how employees contribute to the overall organization.
- Show constancy during tough times—when trouble hits, leadership does not abandon employees.
- Create a culture of mutual trust, respect, and openness.
- Eliminate employee fear of reprisals.
- Focus efforts and empower employees to complete them.
- Encourage creativity, risk taking, and continuous improvement in everyone.

- Mediate conflicts and personality misunderstandings.
- Delegate decision making, foster leadership, and support autonomy.

CHAPTER IMPLICATIONS

- To successfully facilitate an inspirational environment wherein employees can find their peak performance, managers must genuinely believe in and practice those behaviors they are promoting.
- Employees who are given concrete goals, control over their resources, opportunities to make decisions, new challenges to meet continuously, and timely feedback are most likely to operate at peak performance levels.
- Contemporary workplaces have given employees rights and privileges that encourage their autonomy and increase their responsibilities. Employees expect to be treated as professionals, and managers need to be keenly aware of their employees' expectations when facilitating.
- Employees performing in an inspirational workplace culture are typically exemplary—engaged, motivated, committed to the organization, ethical, happy, well-balanced, and healthy.

QUESTIONS FOR REFLECTION

1. Overall, how inspirational is your organization? Are there strategies you might use to create a more inspirational culture?
2. To what extent do you model the behaviors you desire in your employees? To what extent are your values congruent with those of the organization?
3. How do you plan to make the time for initiating, implementing, monitoring, and sustaining those characteristics that engage, motivate, and inspire your subordinates?
4. To what extent do you have the support of your superiors for implementing the strategies suggested in this chapter? The support of your colleagues?

FOUR

Facilitating Collaborative Decision Making

The concept of democracy assumes that citizens should be able to have input into decisions that affect their lives. Similarly, at work, ... important decisions should involve those individuals whose work lives are affected by the decision outcome.[1]

Since the early 1980s, organizations have been taught that the most effective managers are those who use a participative style of management, especially when making decisions. The reality, however, is that participatory, or collaborative, decision making is not something that can be applied in all conditions. Decision making is unique to any given situation, and how it is best accomplished depends on a variety of factors—the manager, the employees, the organization, the time frame, and the decision itself.

In this chapter, we address how managers can effectively facilitate decision making. We're using the phrase "effectively facilitate decision making" rather than "collaborative decision making" purposely, as we advocate that not all decisions lend themselves to collaboration. Initially, we provide a brief overview on facilitating change. Since most decisions imply change to a greater or lesser extent, managers are necessarily change agents. Next, we'll present some guidelines for determining when decision

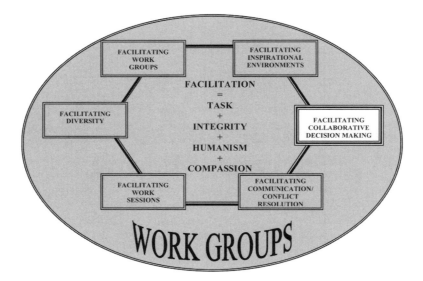

In this chapter, you will learn to:

- Manage change effectively

- Evaluate the advantages and disadvantages of collaborative decision making

- Match decision-making strategies with the decision to be made

- Facilitate collaborative decision making

- Facilitate collaborative problem solving

making is done most appropriately by managers themselves, and when collaborative decision making is advisable. Step-by-step information on how to facilitate successful collaborative decision making and problem solving is included as well.

INTRODUCING AND MANAGING CHANGE

Ironically, the only constant on which humans can rely—change—is the one thing they most resist. Managers are responsible for moving their organizations and subordinates forward and dealing with change daily. Understanding some of the variables that influence mindset and behavioral changes can assist managers in facilitating smoother transitions for their subordinates.

Ultimately, each employee is responsible for adapting to change. There are, however, some techniques that managers can employ for initiating and managing change. We mention four techniques that appear to be particularly effective for working with adults:

1. A purpose to believe in
2. Meaningful reinforcement
3. Skills for adopting change
4. Consistent, positive role models

Purpose

When individuals believe in the underlying purpose for change, they will more readily adapt to change. The operant word in this last sentence is "believe." The purpose for the change must resonate with individuals' values and be consistent with their workplace purpose. Equally important is that they also understand their specific role in promoting this new purpose and believe it is worthwhile for them to uphold.

Reinforcement

For people to both adopt and continue with their new thinking and behaviors, they must benefit in ways commensurate with their efforts to change. Within organizations, this means that reporting structures, operational processes, and measurement procedures—setting targets, measuring performance, and giving financial and nonfinancial rewards—encourage the new thinking and behaviors. Individuals need to receive payoffs that promote their ongoing labors; otherwise new behaviors will be replaced by older, more familiar ones.

Skills

Embracing attitudinal and behavioral changes means individuals must have or acquire certain skills. Adults must be given the opportunity to do the following, or change simply doesn't work:

- Carefully think through and absorb the information.
- Use the information experimentally.
- Integrate the information with their existing knowledge.

Change needs to be broken into segments with time between the segments for employees to reflect, experiment, and apply the new concepts. When they are given the chance to describe to others how they are adapting to the changes, they embrace the change more enthusiastically and completely.

Role Models

Benjamin Spock, the well-known pediatrician, concluded that consistent, positive role models are the decisive factor in the development of children. Research shows that this remains true in most social circumstances, including work. Employees typically model their behaviors after those in positions of influence. Thus, to encourage change within an organization, managers as people of influence must "walk the talk." Employees also change relative to the groups with which they identify; desirable role modeling should be exhibited consistently by those around them if employees are to change.

DECISION-MAKING STRATEGIES

Managers continuously make decisions about their work and their employees, choosing whether or not to involve their employees in the process. If they determine that the decision will be made collaboratively, they must next decide the extent of collaboration. Much of this is dependent on the nature of the work culture; those environments perceiving the manager as the sole authority tend to discount the employees' role in decisions. The converse, of course, is also true. However, there are very real advantages and disadvantages to involving employees in the decision-making process.

Advantages to Collaborative Decision Making

- Groups of employees tend to have greater cumulative knowledge or expertise than a single individual. This is particularly true in today's more complex workplace, which is so heavily reliant on technology.
- Groups, chiefly because of their differences (see Chapter 2 for more details on temperament theory), tend to articulate more values and perspectives representative of the issues and concerns at stake in the decision. Involving employees increases the likelihood that more of the major issues affecting employees will surface and be addressed.
- When employees are involved in the decision making, they have greater ownership of the decision. They care more about the outcome and will work more diligently to bring the decision to fruition. Also, because they understand the rationale underlying the decision, as its implementation unfolds the employees are able to propose alternatives that can avert unplanned and unwanted outcomes.
- The greater the extent of employee involvement in all aspects of the organization the greater their opportunities for growth and skill enhancement. Involvement feeds the employees' sense of professionalism and encourages deeper commitment to the organization.
- One of the biggest deterrents to successfully implementing a decision is employee resistance. When they are involved in making the decision, employees are much more willing to accept it. In fact, they often become the decision's biggest champions, working hard to identify and overcome obstacles that stand in the way of its success.
- Employees typically understand their jobs and their roles in the organization better than anyone else. Although this seems self-evident, when problems arise the solutions are often the decisions of those removed from the situation. When employees are included in such decisions, the results are almost always universally improved.[2]

Disadvantages of Collaborative Decision Making

- In collaborative decision making, employees are encouraged to voice their opinions, concerns, and expertise and ultimately reach a decision each can live with. This kind of participation in the decision-making process takes considerably more time than making a decision unilaterally.
- When groups are asked to participate in decision making, they need the appropriate background and expertise. If they don't have it, the resulting decision will typically be inferior.
- When group discussions are not well structured, more dominant individuals without the expertise can intimidate other members who

may have higher levels of expertise. Again, resulting decisions can be low quality and employees who "participated" may feel resentful.
- If employees are not operating within a general climate of trust and respect, they may not contribute for a number of reasons such as fear of retribution or concern over potential conflicts. Or they may verbally endorse the thinking of those they perceive to be "in power" without evaluating clearly other alternatives.

Matching Decision-Making Strategies with the Decision at Hand

Including or not including employees in making decisions can be resolved by the relative importance of the preceding advantages and disadvantages to the decision at hand. Decisions requiring immediate attention may preclude managers from including their subordinates, as might decisions not impacting them. On the other hand, when managers don't have the necessary expertise to resolve a problem or make a decision, they really must include at a minimum their subordinates with the crucial knowledge.

Managers have essentially seven decision-making strategies under five classifications from which to choose: autocratic, consultative, negotiation, autonomous, or collaborative decision making. Table 4.1 describes the seven strategies under their respective classifications.[3] Any of these strategies can be a suitable option depending on the situation.

Choosing the most effective strategy for decision making requires that managers carefully scrutinize the conditions surrounding the problem or issue. Essentially, managers must consider the time available for making the decision, the expertise needed to make the decision, and the necessity of the subordinates' acceptance of or commitment to the decision. In the following exercise, we list questions that managers can use to settle on the decision-making strategy to employ. Of course, the time available plays a critical role in determining those strategies that are viable options. When considering their options, managers need to realize that the greater the degree of employee involvement in decision making the longer the time obligation.

Decision-Making Questions for Managerial Consideration

1. Is the problem or issue well defined? If yes, proceed to next question. If no, clarify the problem or issue.
2. Does the decision require a high level of expertise to make a viable solution?

3. Do I have the necessary expertise to make the decision independently?
4. Do my subordinates have sufficient information or background to make this decision?
5. Will my subordinates be affected by this decision?
6. Is the subordinates' acceptance of the decision critical to effective implementation?
7. If I make the decision independently, will my subordinates accept and support it?
8. Will I be able to independently anticipate and address all the outcomes resulting from the decision?
9. Am I jeopardizing an open, trusting, and respectful culture if my subordinates are not included in this decision?
10. Will my employees' morale suffer if they are not involved in this decision?
11. Are there legal considerations to the decision?

As managers begin answering these questions, the decision-making strategies that could prove most advantageous to the decision at hand emerge. For example, if the answer to question 3—Do I have the necessary expertise?—is "no," managers must seek assistance from experts. The experts can be consulted, given the assignment autonomously, or worked with collaboratively. For the most part, the manager's "no" response eliminates the autocratic strategies, particularly the first one.

If the answers to questions 5 through 10 (those that deal most specifically with the need for employee acceptance and support of the decision) are "yes," the autocratic, consultative, and negotiation strategies are probably not the best options. A "yes" answer to question 11—Are there legal considerations?—may indicate negotiation as the only viable option.

Contingent on the answers to the questions in the exercise, Table 4.2 provides general guidelines for selecting appropriate decision-making classifications and strategies. These are suggestions only for the manager's consideration. The circumstances surrounding decision making are unique, ultimately requiring the manager's discrimination and judgment. Note: Table 4.2 is designed to be used in conjunction with Table 4.1 and the Decision-Making Questions exercise.

An important note regarding selecting the autonomous classification/strategy: Group members should be well versed in systematic decision making to achieve a high-quality, suitable decision without the guidance of a facilitator. Delegating, which is what this strategy promotes, means that either the individual members or the group is responsible for

Table 4.1
Decision-Making Strategies

Classification	Strategy
Autocratic	a. Manager solves problem or makes decision herself, using the information available at the time.
	b. Manager obtains information needed from subordinates, then makes decision independently. Manager may or may not give subordinates any details about the decision/problem. Subordinates' only role in the decision is providing specific information the manager requests rather than generating or evaluating alternatives or solutions.
Consultative	a. Manager shares the problem or issue with relevant subordinates individually, asking for their ideas and suggestions without bringing them together as a group. Manager subsequently makes the decision, which may or may not reflect subordinates' influence.
	b. Manager shares the problem or issue with subordinates in a group wherein subordinates share ideas and suggestions. Manager then makes decision that may or may not reflect subordinates' input.
Negotiation	a. Typically used in mediation and/or negotiations (e.g., employee contracts), manager brings concerns to the table and decides conjointly with the representative employee group. Process seeks agreement and when necessary mutual compromise between manager's and group's proposals.
Autonomous	a. Manager delegates to either individual employees or work groups responsibility for making the decision or portions of it.
Collaborative Decision Making	a. Manager shares the problem or issue with all subordinates as a group. Group generates and evaluates options and reaches consensus (agreement) on a solution. Manager serves as facilitator, coordinating the discussion, keeping it focused on the problem, and ensuring that all critical issues are discussed. Manager is open to the group's ideas and does not try to influence the group to adopt any given solution. Manager works to accept and implement the group's decision.

developing an action plan. When managers delegate all the detailed planning to group members for managing in their own way, by default the group becomes an autonomous entity with political implications.

Table 4.2
Suggested Decision-Making Strategies (Refer to Table 4.1 and Decision-Making Questions)

Question	Answer Y	Answer N	Classification/Strategy* — Autocratic	Negotiation**	Consultative	Autonomous	Collaborative
1. Is problem/issue well defined?	x		Not enough information to make selection—proceed to next question				
2. Does decision require expertise?		x	Not enough information to make selection—proceed to next question				
3. Do I have the necessary expertise?	x		a or b		a or b	a	a
4. Do subordinates have the expertise?		x	b		a or b	a	a
5. Are subordinates affected?	x		a			a	a
6. Is subordinates' acceptance critical?	x		a or b		a or b	a	a
7. Will subordinates accept and support it?	x		a or b		a or b	a	a
8. Can I independently address outcomes?	x		a or b		a or b	a	a
9. Am I jeopardizing the culture?	x		a or b		a or b	a	a
10. Will employee morale suffer?	x		a or b		a or b	a	a
11. Are there legal considerations?	x		Determine legal ramifications before identifying strategy—could be negotiation. (See **)				
		x	a or b		a or b	a	a

*Note: Before selecting a decision-making strategy, managers must evaluate the surrounding circumstances. In some cases, the most appropriate decision-making strategy is readily apparent; in others, managers need to weigh the pros and cons of including versus not including employees.

**Note: As defined in this book, negotiation is a formal process based on established binding contracts. Thus, negotiation would only be used in certain cases, for example, contract renewals, arbitration, or court-ordered mediation.

Facilitating Collaborative Decision Making

When managers determine that collaboration is the best method of decision making, facilitating the decision-making process begins. Facilitators need to implement a systematic way of reaching a group decision that every member endorses and is willing to practice. Usually, when they understand the method they are using, employees are better able to focus their efforts. We suggest introducing the following five-step process to employees at their initial meeting:

1. Define the decision.
2. Determine the boundaries within which the decision is to be made.
3. Choose who makes the decision.
4. Determine the criteria the decision must meet.
5. Make the decision.

Defining the decision begins the decision making. Establishing clarity about what the decision actually entails is key to reaching a proper response.

Determining the boundaries within which the decision will be made means identifying such things as organizational resources that may or may not be available, time limits, personnel constraints, and organizational and/or customer expectations. Boundaries may be helpful to or may hinder the decision-making process; they must be carefully articulated and examined for their individual and collective impact.

Choosing who will make the decision can be determined next. Even in collaborative decision making, not all employees need to be involved. For example, sometimes a decision has multiple segments and/or requires expertise not shared by all employees. Time may be a constraint and may dictate that some employees work on one decision aspect while other employees tackle another. Regardless of who makes the decision, however, the full group must agree to stand behind it.

Determining the criteria that the decision must meet is the fourth step. These criteria could include desired level of quality, outcomes that have to be addressed, and other such standards. When established criteria are unambiguous, the decision is more likely to produce an effective outcome.

Making the decision is the final step. Decisions are made by setting a deadline and choosing the most appropriate decision-making techniques (we discuss possible decision-making techniques later in this chapter).

Table 4.3 summarizes these five steps and includes questions that are to be answered in each of the decision-making steps.

Table 4.3
Decision-Making Steps and Related Questions

Decision-Making Step	Questions to be Answered
Define decision	What is the decision to be made?
Determine boundaries	What organizational and/or customer support exists for the decision? What organizational and/or customer constraints exist for the decision?
Choose decision makers	Who will make the decision?
Determine criteria	What conditions must be met by the decision? What criteria will be used to make the decision? Who is affected by the decision?
Make decision	What is the deadline for the decision? What decision-making strategies will be used? What is the final decision? How will it be announced? What are the next steps?

Selecting and Using Decision-Making Techniques

When facilitating collaborative decision making, there are a number of techniques available for engaging employees in the process and eliciting their thoughts and ideas. The techniques can be used together or separately, depending on the nature of the decision and the extent of employee involvement. The techniques—Brainstorming, Outlining, Prioritizing, Listing Pros and Cons, Voting, and Achieving Consensus—are common methods used by facilitators across a variety of situations. We've outlined these strategies in Tables 4.4 through 4.9.

Facilitating Collaborative Problem Solving

Managers are continuously confronted with problems needing resolution. Similar to decision making, employees may or may not be involved in the problem-solving process depending on the prevailing circumstances. When employees do participate, managers can facilitate systematic problem solving by initiating the following approach. (This approach is also applicable when managers assume sole responsibility for solving the problem.)

- First, accurately define the problem by detailing the issues of concern.
- Once the problem has been defined, begin gathering both qualitative and quantitative data that can help explain the causes of the problem.

Table 4.4
Brainstorming

Function	To encourage group to develop ideas as possible
Overview	Brainstorming helps groups come up with many ideas in order to consider all possibilities and move beyond current thinking.
How to Use	• Describe brainstorming parameters. • Obtain group support for using techniques. • All participants are urged to voice whatever ideas come to mind without editing or censoring. • No group member is allowed to judge any of the proposed ideas; the point is generating as many ideas as possible. • Record ideas as a visual reminder and stimulus.
Benefits	• Multiple, innovative ideas are produced • Helps participants build on the ideas of one another • Creates openness within the group • Moves group in many different directions to consider possibilities • Breaks habitual thinking

Note: Brainstorming is the most commonly used technique when working with groups that need to generate many ideas.

- Next, determine the most important factors contributing to the problem.
- Then, describe the conditions that you would like to have in place.
- Finally, create a detailed plan to solve the problem.

In essence, by following these steps you're engaging in "gap analysis"— the process of determining what currently exists, outlining what you'd like to have in place, and subsequently identifying where the current does not meet the desired reality. When the "gaps" between current and desired circumstances are noted, a plan that will move the organization toward the situation they would like to have in place is created and implemented.

Facilitators can initiate and sustain a "gap analysis" by directing employees through a series of questions:

- What currently exists around the problem?
- What information is available that we can examine to better understand what is currently contributing to the problem?
- Ideally, what would we like to see happening in this situation?
- What are our options for solving this problem?
- What specific actions do we need to take to move us from what currently exists to what we'd like to see exist?

Table 4.5
Outlining/Flowcharting

Function	To articulate the sequential steps of a process
Overview	Outlining, also referred to as flowcharting, provides a clear picture of how a process works. It is a great technique for helping groups discover flaws, inconsistencies, or other trouble spots in a system.
How to Use	• Briefly define how outlining/flowcharting works.
	• Get group support for using technique.
	• Determine the level of detail to include.
	• Describe and record the process steps.
	• Confirm the accuracy of the steps both inside and outside the group.
	• Analyze the steps by asking the following questions:
	• Where are there problems with the process?
	• Where can improvements be made?
Benefits	• Gives group a clear understanding of a process from beginning to end
	• Helps employees see their roles in and impact on the process
	• Illuminates areas that are problematic or need improvement

Note: This is an excellent technique to use in problem solving. It can be used with groups or individually.

If time permits, facilitating a "gap analysis" is a highly effective way to solve problems. When they facilitate a "gap analysis," managers generally report greater employee commitment to resolving the problem, as they have helped define it and shaped potential solutions. (Beyond problem solving, gap analysis is also a great strategy for improving customer service, streamlining operating processes, enhancing the quality of goods and services, and addressing other strategic goals.)

Examining Decision-Making Success

We've spoken about many decision-making strategies and given steps for facilitating collaborative decision making and problem solving. All of this information is certainly important to successful decision making, but it is only part of the picture. There are certain underlying principles harbored within the decision makers themselves that are equally important to a decision's success.

Making successful decisions is chiefly the result of the decision makers' ability to grasp, understand, and convey important organizational aspects—its values, purpose, and ethics. When these are firmly in mind,

Table 4.6
Prioritizing

Function	To sort the relative importance of the different aspects of a decision and ensure that all aspects are considered before the final decision is made.
Overview	Prioritizing allows the group to distinguish those actions that are more important to the decision than others and determine what needs to be done first before other contingent actions can be completed. It also keeps track of related items that have emerged in discussions but were determined not to be of immediate concern.
How to Use	• Explain the purpose and process of the technique. • Garner group consensus for using the technique. • List all actions that need to be completed in order to make the decision. • Once all actions have been determined, rate each action using 1 through 5:1 = highest priority and 5 = lowest priority but necessary to consider before decision is made. • Set deadlines for the actions in order of their priority. • Assign individual group members to complete the actions, starting with those of highest priority. • Designate a time for discussing the lower priority items.
Benefits	• Helps groups stay focused on the decision by further defining the actions that need to be completed prior to making the final decision • Uses time efficiently in that group has a definitive course of action • Keeps track of all items that are related to the decision and provides a way to add new items that emerge in future discussions

decision makers are guided not by what the organization makes or provides, but by what the organization enables its customers to do. They seek ways that their customers or clients can be served better and/or do what they do better. They listen, capture, absorb, and implement experimentation and new ideas directed toward continuously improving customer service.

Successful decision makers keep the organization's "long view" in mind when creating something new and worthwhile. The "something new" resonates with their values; they regard their organizations as platforms for generating employee and customer excitement and aspiration. They listen to their customers and employees or anyone else that can point to new ways to view and understand the organization's role in their markets and communities, all the while preserving the core intentions of the company's values and mission.

These decision makers are not only ethical in the narrow sense of doing no wrong, but they also go out of their way to demonstrate concern about and

Table 4.7
Listing Pros and Cons

Function	To illuminate the upsides and downsides of decision alternatives
Overview	Listing the pros and cons of a decision option is used to clarify the positives as well as the negatives. Creating these lists for each option can illustrate to the group what they might expect when they begin the selection process. Lists can also assist the group in identifying those aspects of a decision that are more important than others.
How to Use	• Explain the purpose and outcome of the technique. • Gain group support for using the technique. • List the pros and cons for each decision option. • Be sure to record the lists so they can serve as a visual record and stimulus for participants. • After the pros and cons have been elicited for each option, the group can begin debating the relative merits of each.
Benefits	• Encourages group members to analyze every idea and option at least one more time • Focuses the decision-making effort on the results of choosing the various options • Breaks large, complex decisions or problems into manageable pieces • Illuminates aspects of the options that could be problematic to implement

appreciation of the customer's situation. They spend time with their customers (or employees), listening to their problems, issues, and grievances. They consistently look for ways to forge new and more robust connections with the people that the organization will be counting on in the future. They know that decisions made narrowly—on a strictly economic or situational basis—may realize short-term success, but at the sacrifice of long-term organizational goals. Such decisions put the company in the position of being able to realize immediate profit but not to build and sustain relations with customers.

What makes for a successful company is one that strikes a chord with people, sparks their imagination or elevates itself into some kind of special position with its customers. Companies that just make and sell things don't survive: the ones that build and sustain relationships do.[4]

SUMMARY

Making decisions and solving problems are every manager's daily diet. Many questions nourish managers' creativity and feed their resolve:

Table 4.8
Voting

Function	To determine the decision aspects with the greatest support of the group; can also reduce the number of options the group considers
Overview	Voting can be used to rank ideas that are generated during brainstorming. It is also useful as the group gets closer to making the final decision by eliminating options with the least amount of group support.
How to Use	• Explain function and purpose of technique.
	• Gain group consensus for using the technique.
	• Give each participant an equal number of votes (for example, 15 votes per participant distributed as follows: 5 for the first choice, 4 for the second choice, 3 for the third, 2 for the fourth, and 1 for the fifth).
	• If using after a brainstorming session, list all the ideas that were generated.
	• Each group member votes for their top five ideas; they are not allowed to give more than one of their votes to the same idea.
	• Record the number of votes each idea receives; those ideas with the greatest number of votes remain for consideration.
	• If a group member has strong feelings about an idea that didn't receive enough votes to keep as a viable option, that group member is given the opportunity to speak to the idea; the idea may be kept on for consideration if the group agrees.
	• If using this technique toward the end of the decision-making process to eliminate options, the same procedures listed above can be used.
Benefits	• Helps every member participate in the decision, leading to a greater level of commitment
	• Encourages group members to consider and reconsider every idea and option at least one more time
	• Focuses the decision-making effort by eliminating extraneous ideas or options
	• Reinforces democratic principles

Table 4.9
Achieving Consensus

Function	To ascertain the final decision and obtain group support for its implementation
Overview	When all members agree to support a group action, consensus has been achieved. Consensus is not obtained by a majority vote; rather each member agrees to "live with" the decision, including those who may harbor reservations.

How to Use	• Gain group consensus for using the technique.
	• Each group member is asked the following questions:
	  • Can you live with this decision?
	  • Will you support this decision both inside and outside the group?
	• If any member cannot answer "yes" to both questions, ask the following question:
	  • What needs to change to gain your support?
	• All members are asked to consider and discuss any proposed changes. Once discussion is exhausted, each member is asked the questions again. Repeat until all members answer "yes" to both questions.
	• Confirm with the group that consensus has been reached and reiterate the final decision.

Benefits	• Unites group members behind the decision • Helps members learn to work together despite differing levels of support • Fosters interdependence • Forces a decision to be made and implementation plans and actions to begin

How can I solve this issue? Who do I ask to provide input? What are the organizational expectations? How will my subordinates be affected?

In this chapter, we suggested ways managers can analyze decision-making and problem-solving situations, and based on their analyses can select an appropriate decision-making or problem-resolution strategy. We discussed the advantages and disadvantages of making decisions collaboratively and provided methods of facilitating group decisions and problem resolution. We also introduced some techniques that facilitators can use with groups to focus, clarify, guide, and refine their decision-making efforts.

Because decision making is at the heart of the managerial role, we end this chapter with what we've witnessed working as facilitators for organizational and work-group decision making. In our cumulative experiences, those managers who consistently do the following are the ones who seem to always elicit and endorse high-quality decisions:

- Focus on the organization's mission.
- Stay aware of the organization's resources and constraints.
- Remain genuinely interested in the welfare of their employees.
- Intend to do the right thing for the right reasons for as many organizational constituents as possible.
- Be open to honest self-reflection.

Keeping these attributes at the forefront of their mind, these managers epitomize solid, insightful judgment.

CHAPTER IMPLICATIONS

- Managers are by necessity change agents. They must assume responsibility for putting in place conditions that are most apt to making transitions smooth for their subordinates.
- Not all decisions need to be made collaboratively to be high quality. Managers have myriad decision-making strategies from which to choose, depending on the circumstances around the decision.
- Time is one of the key commodities in facilitating collaborative decision making. Managers need to consider carefully time constraints before committing to involve employees in decision making.
- When facilitating collaborative decision making, managers are advised to use a systematic approach. Group members are able to focus their efforts more efficiently when they are oriented to and adopt a methodical process. Also, the resulting decision is of higher quality, as most decision-making systems include all key decision-making steps.
- "Gap analysis" is an excellent strategy for problem solving as well as for improving organizational processes, customer service, and product or service quality.
- In addition to using decision-making facilitation skills, managers need to mirror the organization's mission, purpose, and values as they make decisions.

QUESTIONS FOR REFLECTION

1. To what extent do I analyze the conditions surrounding decisions or problems before making or determining how to make the decisions?
2. To what extent are the conditions that facilitate change in place in my area? In the overall organization?
3. What are some of the lessons I can learn from my previous decision-making efforts? What would I do differently? What would I do the same?
4. What are some facilitation techniques I would use when facilitating collaborative decision making or problem solving?
5. What additional information or skills do I need to facilitate collaborative decision making or problem solving?

FIVE

Facilitating Communication and Conflict Resolution

Not only is conflict inevitable, but it should sometimes be encouraged in order to allow new ideas to surface and to create positive forces for innovation and change.[1]

Dealing effectively with conflict is an essential managerial skill. No organization is exempt from conflict; in fact, managers spend between 20 and 50 percent of their time mediating and/or resolving conflicts. While this statistic may seem discouraging at first blush, conflict is not always negative. It is becoming increasingly apparent that constructively using conflict keeps employees thinking creatively, avoiding mental ruts and "groupthink."

In this chapter, we present information on communication in general and on conflict in particular. We will examine the sources of conflict in organizations and note how conflicts develop. Additionally, we highlight strategies for managing conflict that can increase the odds of conflict generating positive results.

COMMUNICATION SKILLS

Good communication skills are the underpinning of good relationships. Without solid communication, relationships can quickly deteriorate from

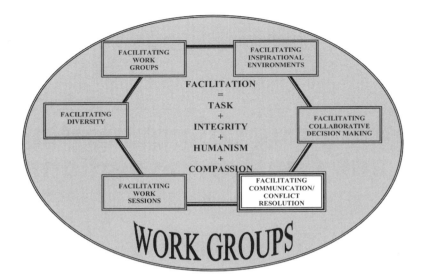

In this chapter, you will learn to:

- Assess communication skill levels

- Identify problems in interpersonal communications

- Recognize the stages of conflict development and resolution

- Assess your and other's conflict resolution style

- Facilitate conflict resolution

feelings of betrayal, distrust, misinterpretation of signals and events, unresolved problems, self-isolation, and so on. Real communication happens when we are as interested in learning about the other person as we are about expressing our perspectives, feelings, and needs. The point is not to make ourselves heard or understood as much as it is hearing and understanding what the other person is "really saying."

To be a good communicator, first and foremost we need to understand ourselves. If we don't understand ourselves and what we're really trying to say, it is nearly impossible to understand others. How willing are we to assume accountability for our actions? What role do we play in communication problems? What do we need to do differently to build trust within the workplace? What changes do we need to make to promote effective communication? The secret is honesty with ourselves as we ask and answer these types of questions.

Practicing Empathy

Developing empathy is critical for managers, particularly when facilitating conflicts. Empathy is "putting yourself in others' shoes" in order to understand and appreciate their feelings, attitudes, values, and beliefs. Empathy requires authentic interest in and concern about others—it is genuinely trying to see the world as the person with whom you are communicating sees it. When you have empathy, you develop rapport where trust prevails so that feelings can be honestly shared; it's a form of communion at an intimate level.

There are some general guidelines for developing empathy:

- First, you need to be honest with yourself about your interest in experiencing others' feelings. If you do not truly want to understand these feelings, if you are insincere, empathy will not occur.
- Remember that communication goes far beyond words. Be sensitive to instances when expressed thoughts and feelings are not congruent. Tune into nonverbal cues—body language, eye contact and so on—as well as verbal ones.
- Listen carefully for the feelings beneath the statements before reacting and forming conclusions. Statements of facts are often misleading, hiding the real message.
- Establish a climate wherein an individual is able to speak the emotional truth that may include negative feelings about you. Be open to exploring negative feedback.
- Use active listening (described below).

Listening Actively

Typically, people only hear about 25 percent of any message. Yet good listening is the single most important communication attribute. When people are listened to, they feel that they matter, are important, have value, have important ideas and contributions, and are empowered. "Active listening" heightens the listener's ability to receive the full message—words and core intentions. It assumes that listening is not a passive activity; rather it requires centering considerable energy on the speaker.

When actively listening, you are paying attention to the following:

- Listening for the feelings underlying the words, as well as to the words.
- Focusing exclusively on the speaker; you're not involved in other activities.
- Creating an inviting, open atmosphere with your body language as well as your surroundings (for example, there is no desk between you and the speaker; you sit facing the speaker in an open, relaxed posture).
- Making eye contact.
- Paraphrasing back to the speaker what you heard to verify that you captured what the speaker really meant.
- Suspending all judgments and comebacks or answers; you are not interrupting or completing sentences for the speaker, assuming you know what the speaker is going to say.
- Not offering advice or solutions; most speakers can arrive at their own solutions.

True communication cannot occur without "active" listening. When you are actively listening to someone, absorbing their point of view and honestly taking it into consideration, you are setting the groundwork for both their and your needs to be expressed and understood.

Measuring Effective Communication

Beyond active listening, opening the lines for effective communication can be promoted by adopting some additional strategies and skills. One way to learn positive communication skills is by paying attention to what makes a good communicator. Notice when you sense that "walls" are put up in your interactions with others. What did you say? What did they say? Observe the habits of those who seem to be exceptional communicators—people who make themselves understood and seem to understand the needs, experiences, and feelings of those around them. Watch for the strategies they use for opening themselves to others and opening others to them.

Because communication is the essence of social interaction—it influences what others think about you and how well they understand you—it determines to a large degree your self-esteem, assertiveness, and social adjustment. No manager, particularly when facilitating any type of activity, can afford poor communication skills. At the end of this chapter, we include a "Communication Skills Assessment" designed to help you evaluate your general communication skills level. Additionally, the assessment includes essential skills for communicating effectively and can thus help pinpoint communication strengths and weaknesses.

Problems in Interpersonal Communication

In organizations (as in most other aspects of life), interpersonal communication problems occur for a number of reasons. Typically, however, the underlying causes can be attributed to six factors: defensiveness, inarticulateness, hidden agendas, status, environment, and hostility.[2]

- *Defensiveness.* Most people have defenses that protect and prevent them from receiving information they fear. Issues that impact values, assumptions, or self-image may be particularly difficult to address; thus defensiveness comes into play.
- *Inarticulateness.* Misunderstandings can arise when message senders are unable to express themselves clearly. If message receivers are unaware of this problem, they may jump to inaccurate assumptions and conclusions.
- *Hidden agendas.* When people have motives they prefer not to reveal, they may send deceptive messages. These senders seek to keep an advantage by keeping the real reasons hidden. Over time, these behaviors cause low trust and cooperation.
- *Status.* Positional authority can distort communications. When speaking to their superiors, those in subordinate positions may craft messages to impress or not offend. Conversely, superiors may "pull rank" and disregard their subordinates' needs and feelings.
- *Environment.* The physical space wherein communicating takes place has a strong influence on outcomes. Informal messages that take place in highly formal surroundings and vice versa can throw off the communication process. Physical barriers such as desks placed between individuals can close off feelings and thwart attempts at mutual understanding.
- *Hostility.* Hostility makes accurate communication very difficult; all messages tend to be negative as little trust among communicators

exists. When trust is low and people are angry, whatever the sender actually expresses will likely be misinterpreted.

CONFLICT IN THE WORKPLACE

In workplace settings, managers are often called on to resolve differences that are impeding the progress of individual employees or work groups. How managers define conflict is critical to how it is received. That is to say, if managers sincerely believe that conflict is a healthy expression of individuals who care about their work, those in conflict are more likely to use it to create synergy. When conflict is facilitated well, employees come to understand that the purpose of conflict is to manifest differences that are integral to their achieving the best possible outcomes.

Stages of Conflicts

To use conflict constructively, it helps to understand how conflicts arise and escalate. Although we are addressing conflicts between individuals or between groups in this chapter (because this is where most organizational conflicts of any consequence occur), conflicts take place at all organizational levels. For example, two different organizations may clash, as might different units within the same organization. We won't go into detail about these types of conflicts, but we mention them so managers are aware that such conflicts can influence interpersonal relationships.

Interpersonal conflicts often develop because of individual differences, such as differences in values, attitudes, beliefs, needs, and perceptions. Conflicts also occur when there are misunderstandings or communication errors that subsequently lead individuals to perceive that there are differences in values, attitudes, beliefs, or needs. It is important to remember that perceptions are an individual's "truth" despite the facts surrounding an issue.

Regardless of the reasons for the conflict, conflicts typically follow a sequence of four stages.[3] In the first stage, the conflict is latent. Neither party senses a conflict, but individual or group differences or organizational structures are creating conflict conditions.

When the conflict materializes and is acknowledged by one or more of the parties, it moves into the second stage. In this stage, individuals become aware of the differences and often react emotionally. Emotional reactions can range from anger and hostility to frustration, anxiety, and pain, or a combination of these feelings.

In the third stage, the conflict moves beyond the cognitive and emotional to action. The conflict becomes overt, and individuals shift toward escalation or resolution. Individuals choosing to escalate the situation may use various aggressive behaviors, including verbal attacks, sabotaging the "other side's" work efforts and/or engaging others in the "battle" by encouraging them to take sides. Actions to resolve the conflict usually require both parties to take a positive problem solving approach so that their needs and concerns are heard and addressed.

The fourth and final stage of conflict is the outcome and aftermath. Actions in the third stage have a direct bearing on whether the outcomes are healthy or unhealthy. Healthy outcomes are those that leave the participating parties with a clearer understanding of the underlying sources of the conflict, an improved decision-making process, increased attention to the needs and concerns of others, and more positive working relationships overall. Unhealthy outcomes include continued anger and hostility, reduced communication, lower employee morale, and other negative conditions. Conflicts with unhealthy outcomes often mushroom, setting the stage for future or ongoing conflicts that are more complicated and difficult to resolve.

FACILITATING CONFLICT

Individuals struggle with conflict chiefly because they lack experience in dealing with it effectively. Most of us have been taught that conflict is negative, particularly in the workplace. At work, prevailing sentiment is that openly expressing conflict is a sure sign of inadequate social skills or poorly functioning work groups. Consequently, when responding to conflict, people run the gamut from avoiding it at all costs to actively fueling it.

Working with conflict is one of the facilitator's biggest challenges; there are several strategies, however, that can turn conflicts into opportunities for employee growth and higher-quality organizational decisions. Initially, facilitators need to examine their perspectives and feelings about conflict. When they are uncomfortable with managing conflict, they can become "caught up" in the debates or not spend the time or resources necessary to bring issues to successful conclusions.

Approaching Conflict

At the end of this chapter, we have included an assessment that can help you and your employees discover how you each approach conflict. When you score the assessment, you'll note that most people have a primary (or preferred) and a secondary (or fallback) approach they use in conflict situations. Although individuals are capable of using any of the approaches, they most commonly use the ones they prefer. Typically, individuals do not make conscious choices about their conflict approach; rather it is involuntary, a force of habit.

Similar to temperament preferences (Chapter 2), there are no "good" or "bad" approaches; however, some will undoubtedly work better in some conditions than others. The key is to understand that there are multiple approaches and consciously make the decision to use the approach that is most productive in any given situation. Having the flexibility to identify, choose, and move among the five methods gives facilitators a powerful tool for interacting with groups. Helping group members learn about and use the various approaches expands their capacity to handle conflict and gives them a common language in discussions.

The different approaches to conflict—Avoiding, Competing, Accommodating, Compromising, and Collaborating—can be represented along the two dimensions of agreement and power. Agreement is the extent to which you are willing to work toward meeting the other party's needs and issues; power is the extent to which you are willing to work toward meeting your own needs and concerns. As you will note in Figure 5.1, the avoiding approach represents low agreement and low power; the competing approach exhibits high power and no agreement; accommodating indicates high agreement and no power; compromising is intermediate in both agreement and power; and collaborating is high in both agreement and power.

The five approaches represent very different ways to manage conflict. Nonconfrontational strategies include avoiding and accommodating, controlling strategies reflect competing, and more solution-oriented strategies are found in collaborating and compromising.

1. *Avoiding approach.* When individuals realize there is a conflict but do not confront it, they are using the avoiding approach. By avoiding, they neither work to satisfy their own nor others' needs. Avoiding can be accomplished by withdrawing (in some cases actually creating a physical separation), by suppressing feelings, and/or by resisting discussion of the issues. This can be a very useful strategy, particularly when there are strong adversarial emotions—avoiding gives people an opportunity to "cool off." In the long term however, if not addressed the conflict is likely to reemerge, especially if it reflects an underlying management issue.

2. *Competing approach.* The competing approach is when individuals work only to achieve their own goals. Oftentimes, individuals employing

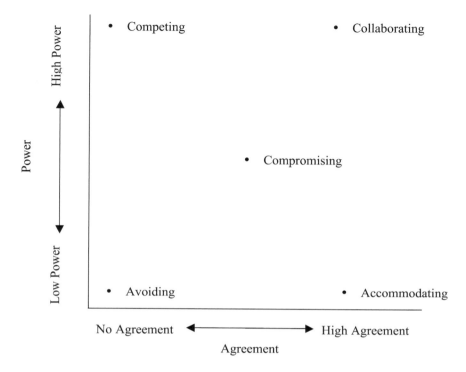

Figure 5.1 Conflict Approaches

this approach will use formal rules and authority structures (representing organizational power) to get the outcomes they want. Although there are instances where quick, decisive action is necessary and competing is appropriate, competing often leads to unhealthy outcomes. Competing behaviors establish a win-lose confrontation where there are clear winners and losers. Because competing is an obvious use of force, some employees can be intimated by those who are more forceful. Generally, this causes a buildup of resentment and a breakdown in communication.

3. *Accommodating approach.* Accommodating is the converse of competing. When using the accommodating approach, individuals are working toward satisfying the other party's concerns at the exclusion of their own. Accommodating can take the form of selfless generosity, yielding to another's point of view even when in disagreement, and obeying an "order" although it runs counter to personal beliefs. This approach can preserve harmony and avoid disruption in the short run; however, if individuals continue to sacrifice their needs over

time, resentment grows, quality decision making suffers, morale drops, and work-group performance deteriorates.

4. *Compromising approach.* Compromising is considered a solution-oriented strategy. Individuals using this approach are concerned both with their own and others' interests and goals and are willing to negotiate to achieve a satisfactory outcome. An underlying assumption of compromising is that there is a fixed amount of something that precludes either party from getting all it wants; something must be split through compromise so that neither party loses. However, because neither party actually wins, some people remain focused on what they had to give up in order to get what they wanted.

5. *Collaborating approach.* Although similar to compromising in that individuals are concerned with their own interests and needs as well as those of the other party, collaborating has no assumption of fixed resources. No one is forced to give up something to gain something else. The assumption in collaborating is that by openly, honestly, and constructively addressing the problem, a solution will be found that will satisfy everyone and where everyone wins. Clearly this approach has multiple advantages to cohesion, morale, esprit de corps, trust, and so on; however, when time is short, collaboration may not be possible as it is usually time consuming.

Advantages and Disadvantages of Conflict Approaches

As we mentioned earlier, each of the conflict approaches has advantages and disadvantages that make it more or less appropriate to a situation. In Table 5.1, we suggest various conditions under which each of the approaches might be suitable. The ultimate choice, of course, will be that of the manager who is most familiar with the myriad variables surrounding conflict.

Resolving Conflicts

Resolving conflicts can be an empowering process through which mutually beneficial relationships are built. The extent to which resolution is achieved successfully is largely dependent on the skills of the facilitator. When facilitators model resolution skills—sensitivity, openness, integrity, and sincerity—in their communications and interactions, they increase the likelihood that others will carry out these traits as well.

We include a conflict-resolution process that we have used successfully in our experiences both as managers within organizations and as consultants to organizations dealing with conflict. Admittedly, these skills take some practice, and novices will undoubtedly meet with some "bumps along the implementation road." They can, however, be mastered for use in even the most difficult conflict situations.

Table 5.1
Matching Conflict Approaches to Situations

Approach	Appropriate Situations
Avoiding	• When an issue is trivial, or more important issues are pressing • When the disadvantages of engaging in conflict outweigh the advantages • When individuals need to let go of emotions that can escalate conflict • When others can resolve the conflict more effectively • When you're not directly involved in the conflict • When all the necessary facts are not available • When the conflict is the result of a larger problem that needs to be addressed first • When there is no chance to get your needs met
Competing	• When quick, decisive action is paramount • When people involved in the conflict don't "respect" any other type of behaviors • When an important but unpopular action needs to be taken
Accommodating	• When issues are more important to others than they are to you • When satisfying others and cooperation are primary objectives • When you are wrong—allows better decisions to be heard • When you want to build "political capital" for a later issue • When you realize your position will not prevail (minimize your loses)
Compromising	• When outcomes are important, but not worth the effort to fight for • When time is short and a viable solution is necessary • When parties of equal power are supporting mutually exclusive goals • When competing or collaborating does not work
Collaborating	• To find a viable solution when both party's concerns are too important to compromise • To integrate the positive aspects of differing perspectives • To gain employee commitment by incorporating concerns into a consensus-backed outcome • To work through feelings interfering with a relationship

Based on information from Kenneth W. Thomas, "Toward Multi-Dimensional Values in Teaching: The Example of Conflict Behaviors," *Academy of Management Review* 2, no. 3 (1977) p. 487.

Conflict resolution begins with agreeing to some underlying principles. These principles are nonnegotiable; facilitators must believe in and practice them throughout the entire facilitation process.

- If we approach conflicts sincerely committed to all parties achieving their goals and meeting their needs, we are mentally prepared to resolve problems.
- When we think "we" rather than "I versus you" and "we all win" rather than "there will be some winners and some losers," we have established the groundwork for enhancing relationships through conflict.
- Resolving conflict effectively and building long-term, mutually beneficial relationships go hand in hand.
- Resolving conflicts successfully will take time and energy and may be difficult at times; however, the end result makes all efforts worthwhile.

The conflict-resolution process has seven steps.

1. Prepare for resolution.
2. Clarify perceptions.
3. Focus on individual and shared needs.
4. Learn from the past and move on.
5. Generate options.
6. Evaluate options.
7. Make mutual-benefit agreements.

Prepare for Resolution.   Creating an effective environment—the qualities you project as well as the space used—is very important for conflict resolution. When the environment is carefully set, you're more likely to reach mutual agreements. When planning the environment in which the conflict will be resolved, consider the following:

- *Preparation.* Do all that you can to practice and project a positive attitude. Keep the conflict resolution underlying principles in the forefront of your mind and commit to approaching issues honestly and openly.
- *Information.* Locate and absorb as much information as you can about the conflict, particularly factual data. Be careful to remain as unbiased as possible by discouraging others from sharing their opinions about the conflict with you.
- *Timing.* Choose a time that is best for all parties involved. If there have been strong emotions around the conflict, allow participants sufficient

time to "cool off" before actually meeting together; ensure that the participants have the time to devote to the process and if necessary secure their release from other obligations.

- *Location.* Where you meet is very important. If possible, pick a place where all parties can feel comfortable and at ease. Consider "neutral turf" to avoid any unfair advantages to any of the parties.
- *Opening statements.* Begin with positive statements; good openings are ones that let others know you are ready and willing to approach conflict with a team-like attitude that focuses on positive ends. Share the resolution process with the group, letting them know what to expect and eliciting their agreement to use the process. Set ground rules (for example, courtesy, respectful comments, judging the action rather than the person). Ensure confidentiality to the parties involved—"what is shared in the room stays in the room."

Clarify Perceptions.   After you've gained group commitment to the resolution process, the next step is to clarify individual perceptions about the conflict. It's very difficult to find solutions to a problem that is not clear to all parties involved, so be sure to clarify the issues:

- *Sort the parts of the conflict.* Ask each party to carefully describe their perceptions of the conflict. Ask each side to refrain from comment and to listen carefully to what the other side is saying. Ensure that all parties are able to present their perspectives without interruption. If necessary, remind everyone about the ground rules to avoid any inflammatory behaviors.
- *Avoid ghost conflicts.* Stay focused on the current matter by avoiding distracting and unrelated side issues. At this point, the facilitator may be challenged to keep the conversations on target.
- *Clarify feelings and values.* Help the parties illuminate what values and feelings are involved. "Active listening" and empathizing are particularly important at this stage. Encourage all participants to avoid stereotyping, accept (rather than judge) the other's needs and values, emphasize with one another, let go of misconceptions, and reiterate that the parties involved need each other to be most effective in their performances.

Focus on Individual and Shared Needs.   Ensure that all parties have expressed all their concerns, values, and needs around the conflict. Highlight those matters that are shared among all parties; this is often the point when all participants realize that they share common needs, values, and concerns. Participants should be encouraged to discuss shared items; realize that they need one another not only to successfully resolve conflicts, but also to collaborate on joint workplace ventures; be concerned about meeting others' needs as well as their own; and focus on "positive" power—instead of "power over" use "power with." Positive power strengthens relationships.

Learn from the Past and Move On. Don't dwell on negative past conflicts; rather seek to understand what happened to avoid repeating mistakes. At this point, facilitators may be faced with a decision—to continue with the current conflict or go back and resolve past differences. If the current resolution process gets bogged down and all facilitation attempts to move the process forward fail, participants would probably benefit from addressing past unresolved issues. Only after the past has been attended to satisfactorily can participants re-engage in the current resolution proceedings. During this step, participants can be encouraged to consider the following:

- Learn from past conflicts and then let them go; forgive past transgressions.
- Think about the other party's intentions; usually no harm was intended to anyone, so move on.
- Remember to not attack the person, rather the behavior; let others know "I'm not mad at you; I'm mad at what you did."

Generate Options. During this phase, participants are encouraged to generate viable solutions. All parties should be reminded to consider the following when weighing potential options:

- Suggest options that are workable for all involved parties.
- Beware of preconceived answers that have not been carefully thought through.
- Listen to and learn from the options suggested by others.
- Make suggestions without passing judgments ("Brainstorming" is an option—See Chapter 4).
- Wait to discuss options until all have been listed.
- Write options down so each is visible to every participant.
- Remain open to all possibilities throughout this phase.
- Think creatively; move beyond current thinking; imagine.

Evaluate Options. Participants are now asked to review the potential solutions in an effort to move toward final resolution. Ways to do this include the following:

- Identify key options. These are the options that meet one or more of the shared needs, meet individual needs and are compatible with others' needs, use mutual positive power, improve the relationship, and are at least acceptable and preferably satisfying to all involved.
- Pare down the list of options by considering all options, regardless of how unrealistic or unconventional they might appear at first, and eliminating those that the group determines won't work, grouping similar options together, and predicting possible outcomes.
- Select those options that have a good chance at being successful. Use selection criteria similar to the following:
  - Ideas must have a good chance of being implemented successfully.
  - No side should have an unfair advantage if the option were to move forward as a solution.
  - Ideas should reflect the culmination of shared input and information from all parties.
  - The option has to include actions that meet shared needs.
  - All parties must agree that the options will build trust and add confidence to working together.

Make Mutual-Benefit Agreements. In this final step of the resolution process, an option is chosen, articulated, and agreed upon by all parties. The result should give the parties a lasting solution to a specific conflict. There are a number of tactics to include in this step:

- Continue to focus on those options identified in the previous step. If the options that remain were evaluated on specific criteria, they will reflect ways to meet everyone's goals and needs.
- Remain attentive to every party's needs and interests.
- Work within the "givens"—those basic organizational and individual constraints that cannot be altered or compromised.
- In the agreement, clarify exactly what is expected of each party. If possible, include individual responsibilities.
- Garner all parties' support and endorsement of the agreement.
- Keep the conflict-resolution process going by using and sharing these skills with others.

When facilitating the conflict-resolution process, adhere to the specified steps as much as possible. However, accommodate the group's need to repeat or go back to a step; as discussion occurs, new thoughts and feelings are evoked that should be addressed. Also, don't move the group to the next step until every participant has agreed that the present step has been concluded satisfactorily.

Facilitating conflict requires discerning between those issues that are necessary to the resolution process and must be addressed, and those that are deterrents to it and need to be eliminated from consideration. It also means that facilitators suspend personal judgments about the "rightness or wrongness" of the parties and the "fairness or unfairness" of options and agreements. It doesn't mean that facilitators ignore their obligation to ensure that the participants consider mutually beneficial solutions; rather they must engage all parties in assuming ownership of and responsibility for understanding and resolving their conflict.

Handling Difficult Conflict Situations

Unfortunately, managers will not always be dealing with individuals who have successfully transitioned to accepting and using appropriate conflict-resolution strategies. While dealing with each of these difficulties is well beyond the purview of this book, we can offer some suggestions for working with more common issues.

Angry participants. It's natural to feel anger; in fact, it's a healthy reaction to circumstances that have somehow violated one's values. However, anger should not govern reactions in a conflict-resolution situation. One way to keep angry individuals from sabotaging resolution efforts is to wait to schedule mutual meetings until after everyone has worked through their anger and hostilities. Managers may need to work with the parties separately, encouraging them to identify the sources of their anger, acknowledge that they feel it, and then determine what would resolve it. This exercise can help the parties move beyond anger and start focusing on what they need from the conflict-resolution process. Also, angry participants can be encouraged to articulate their needs and values on paper in preparation for the resolution meetings, which can further clarify their feelings. Overall, the idea is to defuse the anger positively, using it to build relationships rather than tear them apart. Under no circumstances should anger be ignored; it will only escalate.

Dealing with people who only want their own way. Unfortunately, there are employees who seem to be locked in a pattern of "either your way or mine." Although there is no guarantee that individuals will change from an "I-versus-you" attitude, managers can use strategies to promote more collaborative attitudes:

- Consistently model a partnership atmosphere.
- Clearly state that conflict resolution is a process in which employees need each other.
- Focus on shared needs and shared power.
- Encourage individuals to voice their needs and listen to the needs of others.

- Generate specific options that provide mutual benefits for all, while also meeting as many of everyone's needs as possible.
- Recall times when shared power enhanced the relationship.

SUMMARY

Effective communication skills are the heart and soul of both management and facilitation. As managers, when we are able to build solid relationships with others, we are showing our commitment to integrity, openness, honesty, trust, respect, and empathy. We're displaying that we are secure enough in our self-guiding principles that can we view conflict as genuine opportunities for personal and professional growth. We're admitting that we are not perfect, that we can own our mistakes, that we are open to constructive criticism, and that we need our employees.

Successfully facilitating conflict resolution is the ultimate challenge for even the most talented and experienced managers; conflict is seldom greeted positively, much less addressed successfully. Yet conflicts in the workplace, when resolved to everyone's mutual satisfaction, are linked to heightened employee creativity and imagination as well as better collaborative decision making. Furthermore, conflict is inevitable—managers will continually face it and be called on to tackle it. Conflict is an everyday workplace reality; let's take every opportunity to use it productively.

CHAPTER IMPLICATIONS

- Good communication is an art and a science. There are several strategies that we can incorporate in our interactions; however, using them skillfully and confidently takes ongoing commitment.
- Communicating well assumes several underlying personal and professional attributes. Managers should carefully consider their attitudes, values, ethics, morality, level of integrity, and self-guiding principles as they contemplate their communication skills.
- When managers are able to use conflict constructively to enhance workplace performance, they are increasing the likelihood of stimulating overall productivity and heightening employee satisfaction.
- As with temperament preferences, each conflict approaching strategy—avoiding, competing, accommodating, compromising, and collaborating—has merit. Their appropriate use depends largely on the situation at hand.

- Facilitators using a comprehensive conflict-resolution process are more apt to achieve success in reestablishing positive relationships. Furthermore, their actions are likely to encourage participants to adopt useful tactics in their interactions.
- Although considerable practice is necessary, learning and using strong communication skills and conflict-resolution strategies are essential tools for today's managers. Without these attributes, their success is limited.

QUESTIONS FOR REFLECTION

1. What is my level of effectiveness as a communicator? Where are my strengths? Where are my challenges? What is my improvement plan?
2. How can I encourage my employees to develop their communication skills? What organizational resources can I access? What outside resources might I need?
3. How committed am I to learning and practicing positive conflict-resolution strategies? What kind of organizational support would I receive for using these strategies? What is the organization's attitude about conflict? What about my immediate superior's attitude? What conflict approaches are typically used in the organization?
4. What are the areas of conflict within the organization that are negatively influencing my subordinates? What "control" do I have over these influences? Are there any actions I need to take to create a more positive workplace climate regarding conflict?
5 Where can I improve my employees' working relationships with each other? Have past conflicts been addressed appropriately? How might I best introduce positive conflict-resolution practices to my employees?

COMMUNICATION SKILLS ASSESSMENT

This assessment is designed to evaluate your general level of communication skill. Read the following statements and indicate the degree to which they apply to you.

1. When explaining something (particularly if it is complex), I ask my listeners if they are following me.
   - Almost never
   - Rarely
   - Sometimes
   - Quite often
   - Most of the time

2. I explain my ideas clearly.
   - Almost never
   - Rarely
   - Sometimes
   - Quite often
   - Most of the time

3. I find it easy to express my opinions even when others don't share them.
   - Almost never
   - Rarely
   - Sometimes
   - Quite often
   - Most of the time

4. When I don't understand a question or comment, I ask for additional information.
   - Almost never
   - Rarely
   - Sometimes
   - Quite often
   - Most of the time

5. I find it easy to view things from someone else's point of view.
   - Almost never
   - Rarely
   - Sometimes
   - Quite often
   - Most of the time

6. My attention remains fixed on the conversation.
   - Almost never
   - Rarely
   - Sometimes
   - Quite often
   - Most of the time

7. I find it easy to express my feelings about the matter at hand.
   - Almost never
   - Rarely
   - Sometimes
   - Quite often
   - Most of the time

8. I can detect the mood of others when I look at them.
    - Almost never
    - Rarely
    - Sometimes
    - Quite often
    - Most of the time

9. Even when I have something relevant to add, I will not interrupt what someone else is saying.
    - Almost never
    - Rarely
    - Sometimes
    - Quite often
    - Most of the time

10. I do not assume that I know what the other person is going to say; I'll wait for them to finish before I respond.
    - Almost never
    - Rarely
    - Sometimes
    - Quite often
    - Most of the time

11. When I am speaking, I am well aware of the expressions and reactions of my listeners.
    - Almost never
    - Rarely
    - Sometimes
    - Quite often
    - Most of the time

12. I can readily share my weaknesses with others.
    - Almost never
    - Rarely
    - Sometimes
    - Quite often
    - Most of the time

13. When I am wrong, I can freely admit it.
    - Almost never
    - Rarely
    - Sometimes
    - Quite often
    - Most of the time

14. When conversations turn to feelings, I continue to contribute.
    - Almost never
    - Rarely
    - Sometimes
    - Quite often
    - Most of the time

15. I am open to constructive criticism.
    - Almost never
    - Rarely
    - Sometimes
    - Quite often
    - Most of the time

16. When I have the impression that I might have harmed someone's feelings, I apologize in a timely manner.
    - Almost never
    - Rarely
    - Sometimes
    - Quite often
    - Most of the time

17. When I am angry and someone inquires about it, I feel free to admit and discuss it.
    - Almost never
    - Rarely
    - Sometimes
    - Quite often
    - Most of the time

18. I wait to review all the facts before coming to a conclusion.
    - Almost never
    - Rarely
    - Sometimes
    - Quite often
    - Most of the time

19. When I talk with someone, I try to put myself in their shoes.
    - Almost never
    - Rarely
    - Sometimes
    - Quite often
    - Most of the time

20. When in conversations, I refrain from shouting and from emotional outbursts.
    - Almost never
    - Rarely
    - Sometimes
    - Quite often
    - Most of the time

21. I am careful to include others in a conversation.
    - Almost never
    - Rarely
    - Sometimes
    - Quite often
    - Most of the time

22. I refrain from using my position or authority to dominate or intimidate others.
    - Almost never
    - Rarely
    - Sometimes
    - Quite often
    - Most of the time

23. I am interested in what others have to say.
    - Almost never
    - Rarely
    - Sometimes
    - Quite often
    - Most of the time

24. I am seldom upset if someone disagrees with me, even if that person doesn't have my experience.
    - Almost never
    - Rarely
    - Sometimes
    - Quite often
    - Most of the time

25. When I make a criticism, I make sure I refer to the person's actions and behavior, and not the person. For example, I will say, "I disagree with the system you're using to solve that problem," rather than, "You're wrong!" or "You're not going about this problem the right way."
    - Almost never
    - Rarely
    - Sometimes
    - Quite often
    - Most of the time

26. I am able to resolve problems without losing control of my emotions.
    - Almost never
    - Rarely
    - Sometimes
    - Quite often
    - Most of the time

27. I am aware of my emotional reactions to what is being said in a conversation.
    - Almost never
    - Rarely
    - Sometimes
    - Quite often
    - Most of the time

28. I address touchy topics in a timely manner.
    - Almost never
    - Rarely
    - Sometimes
    - Quite often
    - Most of the time

29. I am able to confront someone who has hurt my feelings.
    - Almost never
    - Rarely
    - Sometimes
    - Quite often
    - Most of the time

30. I voice my opinions and disagreements even when others might get angry with me.
    - Almost never
    - Rarely
    - Sometimes
    - Quite often
    - Most of the time

Scoring

Tally the responses as follows:

___ Most of the time x 4 =
___ Quite often   x 3 =
___ Sometimes   x 2 =
___ Rarely   x 1 =
___ Almost never   no value
          Total

The closer your score is to 120 the more effective are your communication abilities. Noting those statements that received a lower score can help you determine those areas that could be improved.

Note: This assessment was adapted by the coauthor (Whichard) from an instrument retrieved initially from the public domain at http://www.queendom.com/tests/relationships/communication_skills.html on June 21, 2001. Since that date, it has been modified, validated (content validity ~93 percent) and used with approximately 500 people (reliability ~88.2 percent). The instrument was not copyrighted.

WHAT IS YOUR PRIMARY CONFLICT-HANDLING APPROACH?

Indicate how often you rely on each of the following tactics by circling the number that is most appropriate.

		1---Rarely ----| ---- Always---5				
1.	I argue my case with my coworkers to show the merits of my position.	1	2	3	4	5
2.	I negotiate with my coworkers so that a compromise can be reached.	1	2	3	4	5
3.	I try to satisfy the expectations of my coworkers.	1	2	3	4	5
4.	I try to investigate an issue with my coworkers to find a solution acceptable to us.	1	2	3	4	5
5.	I am firm in pursuing my side of the issue.	1	2	3	4	5
6.	I attempt to avoid being "put on the spot" and try to keep my conflict with my coworkers to myself.	1	2	3	4	5
7.	I hold onto my solution to a problem.	1	2	3	4	5
8.	I use "give and take" so that a compromise can be made.	1	2	3	4	5
9.	I exchange accurate information with my coworkers to solve a problem together.	1	2	3	4	5

10.	I avoid open discussion of my differences with my coworkers.	1	2	3	4	5
11.	I accommodate the wishes of my coworkers.	1	2	3	4	5
12.	I try to bring all of our concerns out into the open so that the issues can be resolved in the best possible way.	1	2	3	4	5
13.	I propose a middle ground for breaking deadlocks.	1	2	3	4	5
14.	I go along with the suggestions of my coworkers.	1	2	3	4	5
15.	I try to keep my disagreements with my coworkers to myself to avoid hard feelings.	1	2	3	4	5

To determine your primary conflict-handling approach, place the number you circled for each statement next to the number for that statement. Next, total the columns.

	Competing	Collaborating	Avoiding	Accommodating	Compromising
	1. ___	4. ___	6. ___	3. ___	2. ___
	5. ___	9. ___	10. ___	11. ___	8. ___
	7. ___	12. ___	15. ___	14. ___	13. ___
Totals	___	___	___	___	___

Your primary (preferred) conflict-handling approach is the category with the highest total. Your secondary (fall-back) approach is the category with the second-highest total.

Note: This assessment was adapted by the coauthor (Whichard) from an instrument retrieved initially from the public domain at http://pertinent.com/pertinfo/business/exercises/conflict.html on June 21, 2001. Since that date, it has been modified, validated (content validity ~89 percent) and used with approximately 500 people (reliability ~94 percent). The instrument was not copyrighted.

SIX

Facilitating Work Sessions

People do not mind being led when they are led well.[1]

The work session or meeting room is where the facilitation skills of the effective manager come together. Using group facilitation skills to make the most effective use of employees' time is one of the primary tasks of the skilled manager. Helping groups work together to produce results, make decisions, and resolve conflicts requires a highly skilled and effective group facilitator. Facilitating group outcomes is not a magical ability possessed only by a special or talented few. These skills can be learned, practiced, and utilized by any manager in order to create and facilitate effective work sessions.

In this chapter, we will begin with questions for managers to think through prior to facilitating work sessions or meetings in order to maximize the use of time and insure clarity of purpose for all participants. We also provide a sample planning structure for creating an agenda and insuring follow through on action items and decisions made. We then describe and provide examples of group facilitation skills designed to help effective managers insure optimum participation from all participants of a work session or meeting. Additionally, we will highlight strategies the effective manager can use to balance the process and task functions of the group

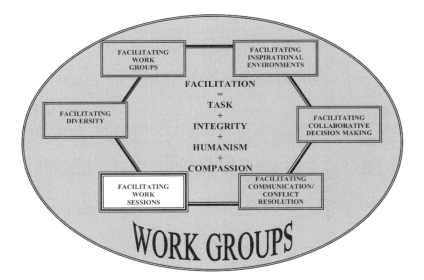

In this chapter, you will learn to:

- Clarify the purpose of the group, plan work sessions, and create agendas

- Engage participants and keep group members focused and on topic

- Balance the process and task functions of a group

- Facilitate difficult situations in groups

- Utilize cofacilitation models

and to facilitate difficult situations as they arise within meetings and work sessions. Suggestions for cofacilitating groups will also be addressed.

PLANNING FOR SUCCESSFUL WORK SESSIONS

In terms of group facilitation, every "ounce of prevention" really is worth a "pound of cure." The more thoroughly managers think through the goals, needs, and dynamics of the groups they facilitate, the more effectively their work groups will function. Below are considerations and questions designed to help managers do the planning necessary to insure quality group experiences and results.

Being Clear about the Purpose

One of the primary reasons groups fail is because of a lack of clarity of purpose on the part of the leader and members.[2] One of the key tasks of the manager in the role of group facilitator is to think through the purpose and goals of any meeting or work session prior to bringing a group together and then to communicate and agree upon these goals and functions with the members of the group once the group has been assembled. Below is a list of questions managers can use to clarify the goals and purpose of the meetings and work sessions they facilitate.

- What are the purpose, function, goals, and/or charge of this group? Who has determined this and how clearly do the members understand the charge?
- What are the purposes and goals for this particular meeting? What do you hope the group will know, discuss, and/or accomplish as a result of our meeting?
- Do you need to meet in order to accomplish these goals?
- Who needs to attend?
- What do you as the leader need from this meeting and/or from this group? What is your role as the leader? What is your attitude toward leading this group?
- Do you have any hidden agendas or goals for this meeting? If yes, what do you want to do with those? Put them aside? Make them explicit?
- Would it be beneficial to have a cofacilitator? Who might this be?
- How might the members feel about coming to this meeting?
- Are there potential problems you can think through or take care of prior to, or at the beginning of, this meeting?
- How can members be involved in building the agenda for this meeting?

- What items need to be included on the agenda for information purposes, discussion purposes, and/or voting or consensus goals?
- What information needs to be distributed to members prior to the meeting?
- How many meetings will you need and how often will you need to meet?
- Should the leadership style and/or facilitator change during the life of this group?

Once the meeting is underway, the manager will want to continue assessing the progress and level of functioning of the group through questions such as the following:

- Is the size of the group conducive to accomplishing its purpose? If not, what can be done about this?
- Is the meeting time too long or too short?
- Are the place, setting, and seating arrangements conducive to accomplishing the goals of the group?
- What are the levels of commitment, goodwill, and trust among members, and between you and the members?
- What can be done to build trust and goodwill between members, and between you and the members?
- What needs to be clarified and addressed in order to increase members' success and commitment to the group's goals?
- What are the interaction and communication patterns of the people in the meetings? Who talks to whom? Who remains silent? Do certain people dominate? Are all participants being heard? Are you as the leader speaking too much or too little? Are the members directing all of their comments to you and/or looking to you for affirmation or agreement?

The time you spend planning and assessing the goals, agenda, climate, setting, and dynamics of your group will pay great dividends in terms of the long-term functioning, success, and autonomy of the groups you are responsible for.

Creating the Agenda

Developing a system for creating useful and clear agendas for meetings and work sessions should be one of the manager's first goals as a facilitator of effective work groups. The "Work Session or Meeting Plan" template shows an outline we have found useful in helping groups create an agenda, track goals, and follow through on action items and decisions made.

WORK SESSION OR MEETING PLAN

Date, Time, and Place:
Persons Present:
Persons Absent:
Others to inform:
Announcements:
 1.
 2.
 3.

ROLES

	This Meeting	*Next Meeting*

Timekeeper:
Recorder:
Other:

AGENDA

Item	*Purpose*	*Estimated Time Needed*
	(Information, Discussion, Action, or Decision)	

 1.
 2.
 3.

OUTCOMES

Decisions Made

 1.
 2.
 3.

Action Items	*Person(s) Responsible*	*By When*

 1.
 2.
 3.

(continued)

AGENDA FOR NEXT MEETING

Date, Time, and Place:

Item	*Purpose*	*Estimated Time Needed*
	(Information, Discussion, Action, or Decision)	

   1.
   2.
   3.

NOTES FOR FUTURE REFERENCE:

Using this type of outline can increase collaboration and commitment of group members by allowing for group participation in agenda planning as well as promoting a system of accountability to each other as members of the group. It also provides a method for improving communication and following through on action items and decisions made from one meeting to the next.

GROUP-FACILITATION SKILLS

Managers, by definition and job description, are group facilitators. Few managers have the training in group-facilitation skills required to do the job however. Below we highlight just a few of the skills needed to facilitate successful work groups and meetings and provide examples specific to work sessions. Becoming a skilled group facilitator takes time, training, and practice. For more comprehensive coverage of the art and science of group facilitation, see the resources listed in Chapter 8.

Engaging Participants in the Group Process

One of the primary tasks of the manager as group facilitator is to insure active participation by all members of the work group or team. In meetings and work sessions, this means using specific skills to engage and invite participants into the discussion, brainstorming, problem-solving, and decision-making components of meetings. People tend to support what they have helped to create. The more the group facilitator can engage participants in the group process, the fewer unexpressed or hidden conflicts may arise later, outside of the group meeting time, to undo what has been decided upon.

Establishing a room or seating arrangement that allows participants to see and speak to each other will allow the facilitator to create an open communication style where participants interact with each other rather than directing all of their comments to, and through, the facilitator. This type of seating arrangement also helps the facilitator scan the group to observe participants' nonverbal communications. In this way, the facilitator may observe participants who want to speak but have not, participants who might agree or disagree with what is being said, and participants who might be confused or withdrawn from the discussion.

Scanning the group is an important skill for the facilitator to master. It requires the facilitator to stay active in the leadership role and observe the group's interaction and communication patterns. It also allows the facilitator to look away from the participant who is speaking and observe other group members' reactions to what is being said. This helps the facilitator determine participants who might want or need to be drawn into the discussion and participants who might be dominating the discussion and need to be redirected. It also encourages group participants to speak directly to each other rather than directing all of their comments to, and through, the group facilitator. This type of interaction pattern can help the group develop a sense of cohesion, an important element of effective groups.

Being aware of the focus of the group is another key task of the effective group facilitator. Good facilitators will consistently assess whether the group is on or off task, whether the meeting time is being used efficiently, and whether the focus of the group needs to be shifted or held on a certain topic, person, or agenda item. Lack of attention to the focus of the group is probably the most prevalent cause of the ineffective use of meeting time. In highly productive groups, the participants will share responsibility for insuring that the group stays focused. This level of functioning usually takes time, however, and the group facilitator will need to assume ultimate responsibility for keeping the group focused, particularly during the beginning stage of the group as it is forming and the participants are learning to work together.

Redirecting the focus and participants in a group is an essential skill that requires tact and finesse on the part of the facilitator. Being too blunt or abrupt can offend some participants, causing them to withdraw from the group process. Not being direct or forceful enough can allow certain participants to dominate the discussion and/or allow the group to remain unfocused or off task. Generally we have found it is best for the group facilitator to intervene quickly and directly when an intervention is necessary. Following are some examples of interventions in which the facilitator redirects the focus and participants in work-group settings:

- One member has been dominating the discussion. The facilitator can use the person's name and directly intervene by saying, "Tom, let me stop you for a second and ask that you summarize the key point(s) you are making in order to insure that others have an opportunity to speak." The facilitator might then shift the focus to the group by saying, "Let's hear from others, particularly those who have not yet taken the opportunity to speak."
- The focus has been shifting to comments and topics tangential to the key point(s) needing to be addressed by the group. The facilitator needs to assess whether these tangential topics require immediate discussion, warrant time on a future agenda, or are unrelated and should be dropped at this time. The facilitator might intervene by saying, "The points you are bringing up are important yet seem tangential to the focus of our meeting. I would suggest that we put these items on a future agenda for discussion and return to the focus of our meeting today."
- Two participants are in disagreement over certain elements of the task at hand. The discussion has been going on for a while and does not seem to be moving in a productive direction. The facilitator can intervene by saying, "Let me stop you both for a moment and decide where we need to go from here. You both have addressed important sides of the issue." The facilitator might want to briefly restate what those points have been and then shift the focus away from these two participants by saying, "I'd like to hear a few more perspectives from others in the group prior to us moving forward with the decisions we need to make and the next steps we need to take in order to accomplish our task(s)."

Making sure that groups function productively is an ongoing task for the group facilitator. Doing it well requires group leaders to be energetic, alert, engaged, courageous, and tactful. Staying aware of the focus of the group and keeping the group focused on their goals has been likened to "herding cats." When group facilitation is done well and the group is functioning at optimum levels, the group leader's role becomes more like that of an excellent orchestra conductor, drawing together each member's finest contributions into the final collaborative product.

Balancing Process and Task Functions

Given the increased pressure to produce that exists within organizations today, it becomes easier to overlook the fact that, as managers, we are facilitators of people as well as products. Balancing the process and task functions of the groups we lead is a higher-level group facilitation skill that can move us from being competent to being highly effective.[3] The manager at this level is a true facilitator, referring to our original definition of facilitation as the sum of task + integrity + humanism + compassion. Task in this equation refers to *what* we accomplish or produce. Integrity, humanism, and compassion are the process functions, referring to *how* we accomplish what needs to be done and *how* we interact with each other while doing it. Following are ways in which managers can strive to balance the human, or process, side of group facilitation while successfully accomplishing the tasks assigned to the groups they facilitate:

- Allow a few moments at the beginning of the meeting for participants to share any news or announcements about themselves or their lives. These might include personal or professional accomplishments, milestones, challenges, celebrations, invitations, or upcoming events.
- Check in with members occasionally during the meeting or work session to see if they have questions, concerns, thoughts, or ideas concerning the task or topic of focus. Ask what they would need in order to accomplish their part(s) of the project or task. Make sure to invite participation from those members who have not yet spoken on the issue.
- Occasionally ask members to reflect on how they perceive the group to be functioning. Ask questions such as these: How are we doing as a group? What else might we add, do, or change in order to function even more effectively as a group of people working together? What do you need from yourselves, each other, me as your group leader, or the organization in order to function most effectively?
- Make time for celebrations within the group. This might include celebrating personal milestones as well as group accomplishments and goals achieved.
- Remember your sense of humor and welcome appropriate humor into the group. Help group members maintain a healthy perspective on the goals that need to be accomplished while being creative about how to enjoy the process of accomplishing those goals together.
- Maintain a few moments at the end of each work session to assess with group members how they thought the meeting went, any final questions, comments, or concerns they might have, or what next steps they will take and anything else they might need in order to accomplish the goals and tasks set forth.

While these suggestions appear simple, time pressures and competitive realities continue to squeeze the process functions out of the equation. Effective facilitators will strive to maintain a manageable balance of process and task functions within the groups they lead, regardless of internal and external pressures to do otherwise. Attention to maintaining this balance becomes even more important as work groups become more diversified in terms of age, gender, ethnicity, and ability. Considerations for understanding diversity in groups will be addressed briefly below and more in depth in Chapter 7.

FACILITATING DIFFICULT SITUATIONS IN GROUPS

It is impossible to list all of the potential difficulties that group facilitators face—what constitutes a challenge for one facilitator may not be challenging at all for another. Below we address just a few of the difficult situations that might arise in a group setting and offer suggestions for facilitating them.

Taking on the Leadership of an Existing Group

Often managers find themselves inheriting leadership roles in existing groups. These groups have established patterns for working together, communicating, understanding power, and accomplishing tasks. Some of these patterns, or group dynamics, are functional and others are less so. As the manager enters the group, the group's dynamics are automatically changed, or at least interrupted. In the role of group leader or facilitator, the manager will want to assess the dynamics of the group early on, working with the group to maintain the functional patterns and changing those less-functional dynamics. The following assessment questions can be beneficial for the manager and the group to consider:

- Who has power within the group? Who takes a leadership role? Who talks the most? Who influences the decisions made? Whose comments or ideas are heard, acknowledged, and acted upon? Who is silent? Whose comments or ideas are overlooked or ignored? To whom do the members look for affirmation, agreement, or taking action? What subgroups or coalitions exist, if any?
- What is the makeup of the group in terms of gender, ethnicity, age, ability, etc.? What differences in communication styles, leadership roles, and interaction patterns might exist within the group based on gender, ethnicity, age, ability, etc.? What does the group want to do about this?
- How are decisions made in this group and who makes them? What are the goals of the group? How well can each of the group members articulate those goals? How successful is the group in accomplishing their goals? What barriers to accomplishing the goals exist and which

of those barriers or roadblocks are set up by the group or members within the group?

- How well do the group members get along with each other? How is humor used in the group? Is humor used to build relationships, reduce conflict, or lighten the discussion or mood, or is it used to exclude, silence, embarrass, or discredit certain members or their ideas? Do the members seem to enjoy working together? Who are the exceptions and why? What might be done about this?
- What gets said or done too often in this group? What is not being said or done enough in this group? What do you find yourself saying or doing repeatedly? What would happen if you said or did something different than you have in the past?

Using these questions to begin a discussion concerning the dynamics of the group is one way to increase members' awareness about the roles they play in maintaining functional or dysfunctional patterns within the group. It also allows the leader to determine how the group functions, what patterns should be kept, altered, or changed, and how the leader might enter into the group in the most productive way. The leader may decide to take a very strong and directive leadership role in order to gain control and make the changes necessary to allow the group to function more effectively over time. Or the leader might assess that the group is functioning well and that the leadership functions can continue primarily in the hands of the group members. Revisiting the norming or renorming stages of the group's process will also be essential (see Chapter 2).

Removing a Group Member

There are times when the makeup of a group is such that the progress and success of the group is compromised. Not everyone works well in a group setting, and at times one or more members may be acting in ways that cause them to consciously or unconsciously undermine the purpose and goals of the group. The group facilitator will want to address this dynamic within the group and also with the offending member(s) outside of the group setting. There will be times, however, when no amount of skill or intervention on the part of the group or the facilitator can resolve the conflict and one or more members will need to be removed from the group. Finding ways in which the member(s) can still make a contribution outside of the group setting is one possible solution, however complete removal of a group member is sometimes the most appropriate, and perhaps the only option left to the group facilitator. Documenting one's efforts at intervention and the outcomes of those interventions is a prudent practice for group facilitators to adopt.

Overcoming Biases and Blind Spots

It is impossible to enter the role of group facilitator without preconceived ideas, biases, and blind spots concerning group members, how
groups should function, and what role the group leader should play.
Becoming aware of these ideas, biases, and blind spots is the first step
in making conscious choices about how one wants to function in the role
of group facilitator. Following are questions designed to help managers increase their self-awareness and improve their effectiveness when
facilitating work sessions:

- We tend to parent based on the ways in which we were parented and
  to teach based on the ways in which we were taught. Similarly, we
  tend to facilitate groups based on our own experiences as members
  of groups. Given this, what have been your experiences as a member
  of a group? What styles of group leadership have you seen modeled?
  Which styles have you appreciated and which styles have not worked
  as well for you?
- When you are leading a group, what types of group members do you
  feel most comfortable with? Which group members do you feel least
  comfortable with? Who talks more in the groups you lead? Who talks
  less? How might you change your group leadership style in order to
  meet the needs of more of the members of your group?
- Do you surround yourself with people who look and sound most like
  you? Do you seek out people who have different perspectives or even
  disagree with you?
- How comfortable are you with being directive and assertive? How
  comfortable are you in relinquishing control and power in appropriate ways?
- What role does your gender, ethnicity, age, or ability play in how you
  are perceived in a leadership role? How does your gender, ethnicity, age, or ability affect how you view your role as a leader? How
  does your gender, ethnicity, age, or ability affect how you view group
  members who are similar or different from you in these or other
  ways?

Effective group facilitators find ways in which to assess themselves
and their leadership strengths, challenges, biases, and blind spots. Periodically asking group members to provide verbal or written feedback on
one's leadership style is an excellent ongoing practice. Using this feedback
to expand one's repertoire of group facilitation interventions, skills, and
styles provides the flexibility necessary to be an effective leader in diverse
and changing work environments.

Cofacilitation

The effective manager will want to consider the potential benefits of having others share in the responsibilities of group facilitation. Cofacilitation models take various forms. Following are just a few suggestions:

- *Shared Leadership.* In this model, the manager would stay in the role of primary facilitator and ask other participants to take on roles and functions such as timekeeper and recorder (see agenda in the Work Session Plan above). Another participant might assume the role of equalizer, making sure that everyone is heard and no one dominates the discussion. These and other leadership roles and functions can rotate from meeting to meeting so that the entire group assumes responsibility for the optimum functioning of the group, increasing commitment and teaching leadership skills as well.
- *Rotating Leadership.* In highly functioning groups, the primary leadership role may also rotate from meeting to meeting. In this way, every member takes ultimate responsibility for the successful functioning of the group, and the power within the group becomes shared as well. With this model, it is important that effective record keeping and agenda-building systems be in place to insure continuity from one leader and meeting to the next. The group will also want to be sure to build in time for the process functions of the group, periodically addressing questions such as how is this model of leadership working for us and how might each of us improve in our leadership role?
- *Mentoring Model.* In this model, the leader would offer the opportunity for a participant to function in a cofacilitator role for one or more meetings. As the cofacilitator's skills and confidence increase, he or she may assume more of the responsibility for leadership. It is important that all interested participants be offered opportunities for these types of mentoring experiences and that it not be based on favoritism by the leader.

The benefits of cofacilitation include helping members learn to share responsibility for the functioning of the group, building members' interest and commitment to the success of the group, keeping members involved and engaged in the group's process and progress, and providing assistance to the group leader in handling the complex tasks of group facilitation. Cofacilitation requires additional commitment in terms of time spent planning with the cofacilitator prior to the meeting, following up with the cofacilitator after the meeting, mentoring and training cofacilitators, and increasing communication between and during meetings. All of this effort can reap long-term benefits and rewards for the manager, the group, and the organization however, and good group leaders find it is well worth the additional time and energy.

SUMMARY

Managers often find themselves in the role of facilitating work sessions and meetings, yet few are trained in the skills of group facilitation. In this chapter we provided just a few of those skills necessary for effective group facilitation and outlined several strategies for clarifying the purpose and goals of your group, planning your group and building an agenda, and dealing with difficult situations in groups. Effective group facilitators create ongoing methods for self-evaluation, soliciting feedback from others, and incorporating new skills and methods into their group-leadership style.

CHAPTER IMPLICATIONS

* Groups do not automatically function effectively. Group-facilitation skills can be used to help group members learn to work together and be productive. Managers can learn and incorporate effective group-facilitation skills to enhance the productivity of the groups they lead.
* Highly functioning groups will need less intervention on the part of the group facilitator. Attaining this level of functioning usually takes time however. Managers can use group-intervention skills to facilitate the group's movement toward the highest levels of performance and autonomy.
* Effective managers always remember that they are facilitating people as well as tasks. Balancing the process and task functions of a group is an essential part of the group facilitator's role.
* As work groups become more diverse, it becomes even more important for managers to develop high levels of competency as group facilitators. Insuring that all voices within the group are heard will increase participants' commitment, understanding, and accountability.
* Becoming an effective group facilitator takes time, training, and practice. Staying open to feedback and opportunities for learning are some of the primary tools of the skilled manager.
* Groups don't work for everyone. Sometimes removing a group member might be the best and most appropriate option.
* Cofacilitation and shared leadership models help managers build autonomous and effective work groups. Sharing power responsibly can increase the leader's, and the group's, ultimate strength, efficiency, and effectiveness.

QUESTIONS FOR REFLECTION

1. What is my level of comfort and effectiveness as a facilitator of work groups and meetings? What are my strengths? Where are my challenges? What is my plan for improvement?

2. What resources can I incorporate to help increase my comfort level and effectiveness when leading groups? What resources exist within the organization? What resources exist outside of the organization?

3. What opportunities for observation and feedback might I employ to assist myself in learning group-facilitation skills? How do I feel about soliciting feedback from peers or group members?

4. What group members' strengths might I draw upon in helping to better facilitate the group? What group-leadership roles, tasks, or functions can be assumed by effective group members? What opportunities for cofacilitation might I create?

5. How committed am I to learning and practicing group-facilitation skills? How committed am I to helping create effective work groups that can function autonomously over time? How open am I to sharing the power and leadership functions within the groups I lead?

6. How committed am I to remaining aware of the process and task functions of groups, maintaining a balanced focus on the differing needs of the people I lead as well as the goals we need to accomplish?

SEVEN

Facilitating Diversity

The way to deal with diversity is not to deny it or ignore it, but to learn about differences so they don't impair communication and successful business transactions.[1]

More and more American organizations are trying to come to terms with the growing diversity of their workplaces. Increasingly, people with very different cultural backgrounds, using multiple languages, are working side by side. Enhancing intercultural communication in the workplace is no longer some future goal buried in long-range strategic plans; it is a real need that exists now. Cultural diversity is the reality, and organizations must deal with it.

In order to facilitate multicultural communication among their employees, managers need to understand that people from different cultures really are different, bringing their distinctive values and beliefs to every situation. These differences, however, need not prevent employees from working with each other successfully. This chapter presents ways to interpret the influence of different cultures on individual behaviors, attitudes, values, and thought and communication patterns. We illustrate how various perspectives play out along "cultural themes"—those underlying tenets of all

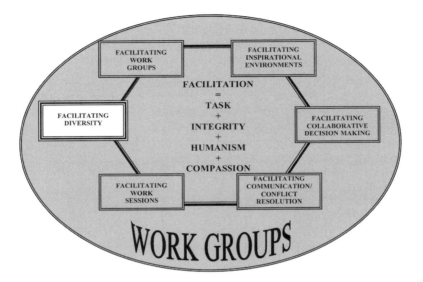

In this chapter, you will learn to:

- Appreciate cultural differences

- Avoid stumbling blocks to intercultural communication

- Recognize and capitalize on gender differences

- Employ strategies to improve intercultural communication

cultures. We'll also reveal how and why so many individuals experience confusion when interacting with others from different cultures.

Before we begin, please note this caveat: The topics of diversity, multicultural communication and intercultural communication (often used interchangeably) are vast and require books in and of themselves. Therefore, our goal is confined to increasing the manager's awareness that workplace diversity is a growing reality, and that it impacts the organization at all levels and in dramatic ways. Although we are familiar with successfully integrating and working with diversity in organizations, we do not have the comprehensive experiences in multicultural communications of many training specialists. Our suggestion is that managers of employees with different cultural backgrounds or doing business with different cultures seriously consider implementing multicultural communication training.

UNDERSTANDING DIVERSITY

Simply stated, diversity is differences. Differences can be as dramatic as those exhibited by aboriginal and urbane views of spirituality, or as straightforward as two individuals from the same culture with slightly dissimilar temperaments. One might suppose that because the United States was founded in large part by immigrants, Americans would be comfortable with and accepting of individual differences. Yet they are as culturally bound as others are to their respective cultures. As Americans, we live within a sophisticated system of commonly held values, beliefs, rituals, attitudes, and so on; we communicate via the English language, use similar idioms to describe everyday events, and salute the same flag. Although we do have our differences, for the most part we are alike.

Workplace Diversity in the United States

In the United States, workplace attitudes about diversity have undergone significant changes in the past three decades. The 1970s introduced more and more women, cultural minorities, and persons with disabilities to the workplace, raising concerns among White Anglo-Saxon Protestant (WASP) men, the unchallenged backbone of American business for centuries. This adaptation, however, has been comparatively easy. The majority of women and persons with disabilities have been American, and the minorities are predominantly acculturated (adapted to the culture in which they operate), thus sharing very similar values, beliefs, attitudes, and so on. Although there are differences, they are made more readily understandable by all that we hold in common. Admittedly, the changes have not always gone smoothly—women and other minorities still experience disparities in positions of authority and salaries from their male counterparts—but generally the workplace is grappling with more sameness than difference. Today, more and more women and minorities, including persons with disabilities, have "climbed the corporate ladder," broken through the "glass ceiling," and are now running Fortune 500 companies.

While we continue to make strides in integrating individual differences into organizational policy and practices, our workplaces still struggle with diversity. It remains a thorny topic despite the fact that more and more employees are working for organizations either established by or residing in cultures other than their own. Far from disappearing from the workplace, managing diversity is one of its foremost challenges. Most importantly, diversity appears to be an enduring trend. Consider these facts from the technology sector, the most rapidly growing area of business across the globe. In 1989, U.S. universities conferred the majority of technology-related baccalaureate degrees to Americans; in 1999, America was third in degree completion behind China and India, respectively.[2] The facts are in: We are a global economy with increasingly global workplaces.

Diversity Begins with Culture

Diversity is a byproduct of our complete immersion in our various cultures. Cultures define our core values and beliefs, our very essence. Each of us is dependent on our cultures to give our existence meaning, to help us define our spirituality and our very purpose. In short, our cultures teach us how to live our lives.

We include a discussion on culture to illustrate how deeply our respective differences are ingrained. It is our contention that rather than trying to make us more alike or to change one another's values and beliefs to conform more with ours, we are far richer when we learn about and respect our differences. In fact, we advocate that differences should be encouraged; our differences are what inspire us each to grow, explore, discover, create, and reach new heights.

UNDERSTANDING CULTURE

Culture is an everyday "given." We take it for granted and rarely examine it. Culture defines a community of people who have shared similar life experiences and interpretations of what those experiences mean. It programs us from birth to death, telling us what matters, what to prefer, what to avoid and how to act. Culture provides assumptions about ideals, helps us set priorities, and establishes codes and justification for behaviors. In short:

Culture is the coherent, learned, shared view of a group of people about life's concerns that ranks what is important, furnishes attitudes about what things are appropriate, and dictates behavior.[3]

But, what exactly does this definition entail?

Culture Is Coherent

Cultural anthropology teaches us that every culture, even those that no longer exist, is complete within itself—it provides an entire view of the universe, including the core issues of cosmology, nature, society, and how humans "fit" within the natural order of things. Throughout time, each culture has grappled with essentially the same life mysteries; however, most have reached different conclusions.

Culture Is Learned

Culture is not genetic—we are not born with it; we learn it. We begin learning about our culture immediately after birth and continue throughout our lives. The important message in this information is that since culture is learned, it is also learnable.

Culture Is the View of a Group

A culture is shared by a society; members agree about the meanings of and rationale for things. Since they consistently practice their cultural norms—language, communication styles, behaviors, symbols, religious images, and national flags, for example—members continually validate their cultural views. Cultures are motivated by common views, and these views are a dynamic force in enabling groups to achieve mutually desirable goals.

Culture Ranks What Is Important

Cultures teach values and their priority. They determine what things are important and their relative levels of importance. Cultural values are particularly strong influences, shaping our attitudes and beliefs and enabling us to evaluate what matters most. Values are what compel people to wars, as well as guide their business conduct.

Culture Furnishes Attitudes and Dictates Behaviors

In addition to dictating our standards of competence and morality, values ultimately shape our attitudes, beliefs, and behaviors. Cultural attitudes, or the propensity of group members to respond the same way to the same object or situation or idea, are feelings based on cultural values and beliefs. Contributing directly to our attitudes, our beliefs are convictions or certainties usually based on subjective and often personal ideas rather than on proof or fact. Our attitudes reflect how important we've judged something to be, how highly it is valued. Although attitudes can be changed, changing can prove quite difficult particularly around issues of importance. Our behaviors follow directly from our attitudes, making our underlying assumptions and motivations more visible and tangible to others.

Cultural Themes

Part of understanding intercultural communication is realizing that cultures share major themes. To give you an idea of the complexity of managing diversity, we're including an overview of those themes in Table 7.1 that most directly influence the workplace. The themes are illustrated as a continuum with the extremes at either end. Each of the world's cultures falls somewhere along the continua and thus exhibits these characteristics to greater or lesser extents. It is important to note that these are generalizations only and are intended to serve as a point of departure for multicultural appreciation. Within every culture, there are subcultural as well as individual differences that further confound our understanding of one another.

- *Universalism versus particularism.* This theme deals with judgments about how best to manufacture, distribute, and market products. Those cultures operating under more universalistic perspectives are prone to view product appeal through low-cost, "one-size-fits-all" lenses, as opposed to the particularist notion of premium products tailored to specific, often unique customer needs. This plays out as very different opinions on how to produce goods and services—mass production with low overhead or individualized production based on customer satisfaction and long-term relationships.
- *Individualism versus communitarianism.* The dilemma inherent in this theme is whether it is more important to focus on the enhancement of individuals—their rights, motivations, rewards, capacity, and attitudes—or pay more attention to the advancement of whole communities, which all its members are pledged to serve. Within the workplace, the way work groups are formed, managed, and performed is influenced considerably by how the members fall along this continuum.
- *Specificity versus diffusion.* This theme illuminates the differences in how to view phenomena (for example, projects or tasks). Is it better

to analyze phenomena, reducing them to specific components such as items, tasks, or units (specificity), or are we better served by integrating and configuring phenomena into diffuse patterns, relationships, and larger contexts (diffusion)?

- *Neutral versus affective.* In this theme, we consider the extent to which emotions should be dealt with and expressed. Do we communicate personal feelings in open meetings and try to engage group members in sharing their feelings (affective) or should we behave more dispassionately, more "professionally," remaining aloof and focus exclusively on the tasks to be completed (neutral)?
- *Achieved status versus ascribed status.* This theme refers to how employees are viewed and rewarded. Are rewards confined to how well employees perform along specific, objective organizational criteria (achieved) or are other characteristics—employee rights, seniority, ethnicity, gender, connections, and so on—important to the evaluation equation? To what extent should the employees' unique circumstances influence their success in the workplace (ascribed)?
- *Inner direction versus outer direction.* In this theme, we indicate how we are guided—by our inner convictions, our conscience, and moral compass (inner) or by signals from the wider social and physical environment into which we must fit (outer). This theme also defines the extent to which people's fates rest in their own hands or in some wider system. Do we believe in self-determination (inner) or is our destiny preplanned and we're simply playing it out (outer)?
- *Sequential time versus synchronous time.* This dimension speaks to our respective concepts of time. Is it more important to do things fast, minimizing wasted efforts and thus saving time (sequential), or should efforts be coordinated so activities can evolve harmoniously (synchronous)? Viewed another way, fast sequences usually are quicker in the short term, but good synchronization can shorten the overall race by performing operations simultaneously that can later be integrated. The questions become, "How and where do we begin?" and "How should it progress?"
- *Linear thinking versus circuitous thinking.* Thought processes are illustrated in this theme. Linear thinking is highly reliant on induction and empiricism (the scientific method), and is very distrustful of abstractions and intuition. Linear thinking depends on words to make meanings explicit. Circuitous thinking stresses the harmony between the whole and its parts. It relies on intuition to inform judgments and is highly dependent on its surrounding context. Few words are used to describe thoughts arrived at circuitously; meaning is embedded in the cultural context.

Table 7.1
Continua of Cultural Themes

Universalism	Particularism
(rules, codes, laws, and generalizations)	(exceptions, special circumstances, unique relationships)

This theme covers judgments about how best to manufacture, distribute, and market products—mass production or specialized development.

Individualism	Communitarianism
(personal freedom, human rights, competitiveness)	(social responsibility, harmonious relations, cooperation)

This theme determines whether it is more important to focus on the enhancement of individuals or on the advancement of whole communities.

Specificity	Diffusion
(reductive, analytic, objective)	(holistic, elaborative, synthetic, relational)

This theme defines phenomena—it determines if it is better to analyze phenomena or to integrate them into contexts.

Neutral	Affective
(dispassionate, controlled, detached)	(enthusiastic, responsive, passionate)

This theme considers the extent to which emotions should be dealt with and expressed—kept hidden or openly expressed.

Achieved status	Ascribed status
(what you've done, your track record, your earned title)	(who you are in the cultural hierarchy, your potential, connections)

This theme refers to how employees are rewarded—are rewards confined to how well they perform objective criteria, or are other characteristics important to the equation?

Inner direction	Outer direction
(conscience and convictions are located within the individual)	(exemplars and influences are located externally)

This theme deals how we are guided—by our inner convictions or by wider social and physical environments.

Sequential time	Synchronous time
(time is sequential, a race along a set course, finite and steadfast)	(time is composed of multiple simultaneous events, coordinated by ever-changing influences)

This theme speaks to our attitudes toward time—should we do things quickly to save time, or should efforts be coordinated and evolve harmoniously?

Linear thinking	Circuitous thinking
(logical, procedural, reasoned)	(perceptual, contextual, implicit)

This theme illustrates thought processes—linear thinking uses induction and empiricism, whereas circuitous thinking stresses harmony between the whole and its parts and relies on intuition.

Fons Trompenaars and Charles Hampden-Turner, *Managing People Across Cultures* (West Sussex, England: Capstone Publishing, Ltd., 2004), pp. 108–9.

Cultural Differences in Management Approaches

Western (for example, U.S., Canadian, Australian, German, French, and UK) and Eastern (for example, Japanese, Chinese, Korean, Indian, and some Middle Eastern) cultures reside in very different conceptual worlds. (Note: Once again, these are generalizations provided only to illustrate broad-based differences; they are not intended as substitutes for comprehensive multicultural training.) Whereas Americans, for example, view responsible individuality and autonomy as personal virtues, the Japanese regard individuality as a sign of professional immaturity. Moreover, autonomy in Japan means the freedom to comply with one's obligations and duties.

In most Eastern cultures, males are born into intricate systems of obligations and relationships. They are expected to remain "inconspicuous" in the workplace, to practice selflessness, to never bring shame to self or family and to always "save face."

On the other hand, females in Eastern cultures, particularly the traditional cultures, have less straightforward roles. Although they have positions of authority in the workplace, their status is still below that of males in comparable positions. They have less "social freedom," although they can pursue education and accumulate their own wealth. As an example, an Eastern female CEO would never appear at an evening dinner without a chaperone; her behaviors are strictly dictated by her male family members.

In Table 7.2, we've highlighted some major differences between Western and Eastern cultures in their approaches to workplace management. Overall, Western cultures perpetuate a competitive workplace environment, rewarding individuals on their specific achievements and holding individuals accountable for organizational successes and failures. Western culture employees work under tenuous conditions; there is very little promise of job security or long-term employment. Consequently, Western employees may feel very little loyalty to their organizations.

> At one point in her career, Judy Whichard worked for Sumitomo Bank of California, an organization almost entirely composed of Japanese employees. There was a common saying in the workplace: "He who tries to be the highest nail gets hammered down." This is a wonderful example of valuing a community above the individual—a cultural preference for communitarianism.

Eastern cultures rely much more on a consensus-building system, involving numerous group meetings and a great deal of time before making decisions. In countries such as Japan, permanent employment is highly desirable; however, it is reserved for male employees in government and large businesses who have attended the "best universities." There is great initial competition for these positions; yet once they have been obtained,

Table 7.2
Differences in Western and Eastern Management Approaches

	Western Orientation	*Eastern Traditional Orientation*
Employment Tenure	• Employment is short term and market driven. • Individual performance is primary to employee evaluation. • Majority of employees have little "job security." • Promotions can be made from within or from outside the organization. • Employee loyalty is to self, rather than the organization.	• Employment is long term and career oriented. • Group performance is considered the chief indicator of employee success. • Once hired, workers have jobs for life. • Promotions are from within the organization. • Employee loyalty is to the organization.
Management Styles	• Managers are typically action oriented and focused on short-term benefits. • Project outcomes are valued over process. • Managers rely on hierarchical authority.	• Managers concentrate on perfectionism for the long term. • Project process is as important as the outcome. • Management relies on group consensus.
Management Values	• Require openness and accountability from their employees. • Believe that time is not to be wasted; may sacrifice outcome if time can be saved. • Prefer employees to be independent; don't need to be consulted on every step of the process. • Employee accomplishments are seen as direct reflection of their management skills.	• Prefer harmony and consensus among their employees. • Time is important, but not as important as a quality outcome. • Like to be informed regularly of progress toward group goals; may even participate in group meetings. • Accomplishments are not attributed to individuals or to management; seen as a reflection of organizational quality.
Reporting Structures	• Formalized and explicit. • Employee expected to hold self accountable for following rules and regulations. • Employee held to position responsibilities.	• Not formalized, implicit. • Group monitors progress and works with looser guidelines to achieve goals. • Group encouraged to find new ways to approach business.
Women in the Workplace	• Women's status is professedly equal to that of men. • A woman's behavior is her own responsibility.	• Women's position is assumed to be behind men. • A woman's behavior is viewed as the responsibility of her male family and clan members.

Table 7.2 Continued.

	Western Orientation	*Eastern Traditional Orientation*
	• A woman's dress and appearance is usually what she wants, likes, and is most comfortable in. • Women can occupy any rung of the "corporate ladder." • Women's behavioral norms are almost all legislated (e.g., equal opportunity and gender equity).	• A woman's dress and appearance are regarded as a reflection of her character. A woman in immodest or revealing clothes brings shame to herself and her family since her attire is considered too conspicuous and inviting to men.
Workplace Protocol	• Outgoing, friendly expressions are highly desirable qualities. • Greetings are extended to all; emphasis is on informality most of the time. • Although some formal protocol exists in certain situations, majority of interactions do not stand on ceremony.	• Outgoing, friendly behaviors are frequently regarded as flippant and undignified. • Greetings are given only to select people; emphasis is on formality most of the time. • Social interactions are governed strictly by protocol, with a keen awareness of vertical social and business hierarchies in one's relationships. The following are true primarily in Middle Eastern countries:
Religion in the Workplace	• Religious values and beliefs are strictly personal, rarely referred to in daily interactions. • Society usually views integrity, ethics, and proper behavior as individual character traits not necessarily linked to one's atheistic or religious beliefs. • People regard themselves as the catalysts for their accompliments and successes in life. • People operate under the assumption of a clear separation of church and state.	• Religious norms and beliefs are often publicly affirmed and quoted in daily interactions. • Society frequently links integrity, ethics, and proper behavior to the degree of one's atheistic or religious beliefs. • People regard what happens in life as an expression of God's will. • The majority of political, economic, and social structures are founded on religious principles.

Lea P. Stewart, "Japanese and American Management: Participative Decision Making," in *Intercultural Communication: A Reader,* 4th Ed., ed. Larry A. Samovar and Richard E. Porter (Belmont, CA: Wadsworth Publishing Company, 1985), pp. 186–89; Fathi S. Yousef, "North Americans in the Middle East," in *Intercultural Communication: A Reader,* 4th Ed., ed. Larry A. Samovar and Richard E. Porter (Belmont, CA: Wadsworth Publishing Company, 1985), pp. 78–85.

the companies are assured of lifelong loyalty and commitment from their employees. For their part, the employees are guaranteed employment and benefits throughout their working lives and into their retirements.

Typical Reactions to Unfamiliar Cultures

When individuals are faced with unfamiliar cultures, there are a number of ways they can respond.[4] Ideally, we would all eagerly explore our differences openly without passing judgment or experiencing anxiety. Unfortunately, unless we are seasoned veterans of multicultural interactions, we may react in ways that inhibit, even damage our communications with others. Some of the more common reactions to cultures with which we are unacquainted include:

- *Assumption of superiority.* This is a universal response to cultural differences, "Of course they're different, but we're better." This response minimizes differences, making them unimportant compared to one's own culture. Most cultures assume their own values and practices are superior to those of the rest of the world.
- *Tendency to evaluate.* When we meet members of other cultures, we tend to approve or disapprove of their statements and actions, rather than trying to understand them through their world view.
- *Ethnocentrism.* People everywhere tend to assume that their own culture is right and normal and to assess all other cultures by how closely they resemble their own. Most people, especially those with little experience of other cultures, believe that their own culture (ethnicity) is at the center of the human experience—hence "ethnocentrism." Alongside preference for cultures that are similar to our own is the view that difference is dangerous, perhaps even wrong.
- *Assumptions of universality.* Regardless of our look-alike facades, assuming that individuals from different cultures are similar is a serious stumbling block to intercultural communication. People are not alike underneath; people come from very different orientations. To assume we know someone else is called "projection." We project when we assume that someone else's perceptions, judgments, attitudes, and values are like our own.
- *Reliance on preconceptions and stereotypes.* Stereotypes help us reduce the threats of the unknown by making our world predictable. This is one of the basic functions of culture: to lay out a predictable world in which the individual is firmly grounded. However, stereotypes prevent us from really understanding one another. Not only do they interfere with our ability to objectively view events, but also they self-perpetuate because we tend to selectively view only those actions that support our stereotypes.
- *High anxiety.* The presence of anxiety or tension is common in intercultural experiences because of the number of uncertainties brought about by unfamiliar customs, foods, languages, interactions,

perceptions, and so on. Regardless of who initiates anxiety, anxious feelings usually permeate all parties in any dialogue, impeding any attempts to understand one another.

Learning about Other Cultures

Undoubtedly, the time will come when you will either want to or need to learn about another culture in some depth. To guide your learning about cultural differences, we suggest you use the following questions. When you understand the priorities people have, you can predict with some confidence how they will probably respond in situations.

- How do people in this culture think and know?
- What is the relation of members of this culture to time and spiritual issues?
- How do they see the individual self in relation to the rest of the culture?
- How is their society organized?
- What do they consider achievement?

While insights into various cultures are enriching and inspiring, they can also be confusing and troubling. Misinterpretations often lead to misunderstandings that create anxiety, a tendency for us to retreat to what is more familiar, or to attach "rightness and wrongness" to behaviors. What we don't understand we mistrust, and rather than trying to breach gaps in interactions and relationships, we distance ourselves from one another.

However, understanding various cultures is proving essential to organizations. When organizations know what other cultures value and understand their attitudes, they optimize their business opportunities. Furthermore, today's businesses are increasingly multicultural; there is no way to avoid addressing individual and cultural differences. No organization can afford to believe that members of different cultures are all seeking to conform to one culture, or that differences will cease to exist sometime in the future. An organization's success hinges on finding ways for people who think differently to work together.

We conclude this section with a list of strategies that can help maximize the effectiveness of multicultural interactions. "Multicultural Communication Strategies" includes some guidelines for assuming an open attitude when building relationships with others from different backgrounds.

Multicultural Communication Strategies

- Understand your own feelings about diverse workers. Examine your inner beliefs and evaluate your level of effectiveness in accepting and managing differences.
- Regardless of their position in the organizational hierarchy, treat everyone respectfully and as your equal.
- Recognize that cultural differences exist, but confirm these differences before you act on them. Don't act on your assumptions; rather get to know the person.
- Stick to the business at hand until you have established mutual understanding. Avoid personal conversations until you have gotten to know one another.
- Avoid stereotyping both cultures and individuals. Stereotyping prevents you from learning about a culture and getting to know someone. Remember that individuals are unique within any culture.
- Learn as much as you can about a culture prior to your interactions with one of its members.
- Consider the feelings, thoughts, and experiences of others, particularly those who are culturally different. Listen and care about what they are saying.
- Seek to find common ground between yourself and others, particularly those who are culturally different. You will often have much in common with someone from a different culture. Be careful, however, of making assumptions about similarities based on appearances; substantiate your sameness through communications.
- Refrain from assuming that a culturally different person is an "expert" about his/her cultural group. Don't ask them to speak for their entire culture; one person's actions do not mean that all members think, feel, and act accordingly.
- Avoid "talking down" to people from other cultures. Assume that they are able to clarify in their own way whatever they don't comprehend.
- Engage in genuine rapport. Be open to and respectful of cultural differences. Multicultural exchanges need not be stressful; generally, all parties are interested chiefly in developing positive relationships.
- Remember that it is not enough to teach mainstream workers to get along with those from other cultures; individuals from other cultures need to be taught to get along with the mainstream workers.
- Be patient with change. Change is usually accomplished in small increments. Acknowledge these increments while supporting ongoing change efforts.

GENDER DIFFERENCES

Within the past three decades, organizations have shown a growing interest in finding and promoting their employees' inherent talents and interests, believing that when individuals highlight their strengths, their productivity increases. One spin-off of this focus on strengths is that organizations are currently using the cultural differences between women and men to enhance their everyday operations. Without stereotyping or judging either gender, and admitting a significant overlap in how both men and women feel and behave—we are fundamentally more similar than different—there are cultural differences in how the genders communicate. The differences can be stumbling blocks to cooperation if we do not understand them, but they can also unlock energy and creativity in one another when we do. Here are some of these patterns. We encourage you to not only become aware of them, but also to look at how the differences might be used effectively in workplace situations.

- Women tend to ask more questions than men.
- Men tend to offer solutions before empathy; women tend to do the opposite.
- Women are more likely to ask for help when they need it than men are.
- Men tend to communicate more competitively and women more cooperatively.
- To establish trust with one another, women tend to self-disclose while men focus on reliability and solidarity.
- Women are generally more sensitive than men to social cues.
- Women will make more eye contact with their conversant and hold that contact longer than men do.
- Women reveal their emotions in facial expressions more so than men.
- Women smile more readily than men.

SUMMARY

In this chapter we have provided a brief glimpse into the complexities of multiculturalism. We've shown that regardless of its level of sophistication or how long it has existed, culture is deeply ingrained in every individual and that life is virtually nonexistent without it. We've learned that all cultures share commonalities:

- Every culture has its own internal coherence, integrity, and logic. Every culture is an intertwined system of values and attitudes, beliefs and norms that give meaning and significance to both individual and collective identity.

- No one culture is inherently better or worse than another. All cultural systems are equally valid as variations on the human experience.
- All persons are to varying degrees culturally bound. Every culture provides its members with some sense of identity, some regulation of behaviors, and some sense of personal place in the overall scheme of things.

We've also touched on the idea that diversity is more than token representatives from different cultures, age groups, and gender, with a few persons with disabilities thrown in for good measure. It's a lifetime commitment and connection to the world's communities, encouraging their uniqueness and enjoying and learning from our differences.

The first step in effective intercultural communication is the understanding and acceptance of differences. That does not mean we have to agree with another culture's viewpoint, or that we have to adopt another culture's values. Nor does it mean turning one's back on one's own culture or denying its priorities. Rather, it means learning what motivates others and how other cultural priorities inform the behavior, attitudes, and values of business colleagues. It also means we and they examine our and their priorities and determine how we all can best work together, despite our differences. It means adding to one's own culture, not subtracting from it.

CHAPTER IMPLICATIONS

- Cultures define their individual members, dictating their values, beliefs, attitudes, and behaviors. Cultures are deeply ingrained within each of us, often making behavioral changes difficult.
- No culture is inherently better or worse than another. This doesn't mean we have to agree with or even like another culture's every aspect. However, it does mean we suspend personal judgments and seek to understand one another's cultural perspectives.
- Every culture shares common themes that can help us explain our different approaches to the way we live our lives and practice business.
- Management styles are dependent on cultural orientation. Differences are particularly evident when comparing and contrasting Western and Eastern cultures.
- Organizations that have proven successful in one culture often adopt an ethnocentric position: We know how to make it work for us at

home, so we can make it work for us anywhere. This could not be further from the truth.

- Those organizations and their employees that have participated in multicultural training have found it not only informative and helpful in understanding one another, but also personally and professionally enriching.

QUESTIONS FOR REFLECTION

1. Does senior management support a comprehensive diversity initiative by providing adequate funding and staffing?
2. Are there multicultural senior managers in important areas of the organization?
3. Do our internal and external communications reflect an atmosphere of inclusion?
4. Are diversity initiatives tied to incentives and performance reviews?
5. To what extent do you need to consider implementing multicultural training in your workplace? If you decide to implement training, what level of organizational support will you receive? What strategies might you use to encourage a higher level of management and/or organizational support?
6. How comfortable are you in accepting and managing diversity among your employees? What resources might you need to facilitate diversity among your employees?

EIGHT

Resources for Facilitators

The people who come to be masters of management do not see their work environment only in structured, analytic ways. Instead, they also have the capacity to see it as a complex, dynamic system that is constantly evolving…. As one set of conditions arises, they focus on certain cues that lead them to apply a very analytic and structured approach. As these cues fade, they focus on new cues of emerging importance and apply another frame, perhaps being very intuitive and flexible. At another time they may emphasize the overall task, and at still another they may focus on the welfare of a single individual.[1]

Daily, organizations encounter new situations requiring finesse, creativity, and refined strategic thinking often under the pressures of time and quickly changing circumstances. Managers are repeatedly involved in making choices about how to respond best to external conditions such as new customer demands, competitive threats, economic downturns, political developments, and a whole host of other business-related issues. Within their organizations, at the very least managers are expected to create new ways to work more efficiently as well as to integrate their employees and reactive methods into everyday business practices.

Fortunately, managers do not need to operate in isolation nor assume the full mantle for organizational success; they have workers who are better educated and more independent than ever before, capable of stimulating solutions and completing projects in record time. Reciprocally, these workers need managers who can invigorate their drive and creativity, spotlight their talents and energies, and garner the resources they require for accomplishing their goals. Increasingly, the most successful managers serve as catalysts, defining organizational outcomes around which their employees first rally, then organize, and finally combine their individual talents until the projects are accomplished. In short, using a variety of tools and techniques managers facilitate organizational vitality by keeping their workers included, excited, committed, and energized.

Throughout this book, we have introduced and illustrated the myriad aspects of facilitation, one of the most valuable management skills. Both an art and a science and mastered only through conscientious practice, facilitation is a keystone of exemplary management. At its most artistic, facilitation is the germinating, ferreting out, melding, honing, and ultimately propelling of individual and group expertise to the successful completion of the tasks at hand while at the same time creating and maintaining a stimulating, satisfying work environment. It is a science in its emphasis on studying individual and group behavioral patterns; understanding and practicing positive communication essentials; implementing systematic problem-solving, decision-making, and conflict-resolution methods; soliciting feedback and using this feedback to modify plans; and encouraging the application of methodology in general.

At the book's onset, we promised an "off-the-shelf, functional, straightforward" resource to help managers, supervisors, organizational change agents, and consultants interact most effectively with their colleagues and employees in accomplishing organizational tasks. To a significant extent, we believe that we have made good on this promise. We have introduced what we consider to be the primary components of facilitation:

- Establishing, maintaining, and monitoring successful work groups
- Creating inspiring workplaces to enhance employee satisfaction and productivity
- Implementing collaborative decision making
- Practicing effective communication techniques and resolving conflicts successfully
- Facilitating effective work sessions and meetings
- Understanding and capitalizing on diversity in the workplace

We have also explained how to develop and implement these components. Throughout the chapters, we have provided assessment instruments, step-by-step directions, suggestions for applying the various principles and strategies, and questions to guide managers in better understanding their organizational environment.

However, as with any book, while this one can certainly provide guidance and coaching in facilitating, it is nonetheless only a partial view of a much larger picture. Similar to management theories and best practices, facilitation is evolving, and we believe it will continue to do so, particularly as workplaces become increasingly diverse, economies more global, and markets more competitive. Thus, in this chapter we are including resources that augment the topics covered in this book. The listed sources have been selected to help readers not only expand their knowledge of the various subjects, but also to stimulate thinking about areas not covered. For ease of reference, the sources are listed by chapter and when applicable the themes within each chapter.

CHAPTER 1: THE EVOLVING MANAGERIAL ROLE

Organizational Trends

Becker, B. E., M. S. Huseld, and D. Ulrich. *The HR Scoreboard: Linking People, Strategy, and Performance.* Cambridge, MA: Harvard Business School Press, 2001.

Buckingham, Marcus and Curt Coffman. *First, Break All the Rules: What the World's Greatest Managers Do Differently.* New York: Simon & Schuster, 1999.

deSoto, Henrio. *The Mystery of Capital: Why Capitalism Triumphs in the West and Fails Everywhere Else.* New York: Basic Books, 2004.

Heet, J., "America and the Coming Global Workforce." *American Outlook* VII, no. 1 (2004), pp. 29–33.

Reich, Robert B. *I'll Be Short: Essentials for a Decent Working Society.* New York: Alfred A. Knopf, 2002.

CHAPTER 2: FACILITATING WORK GROUPS

Temperament Theory

Buckingham, Marcus and Donald O. Clifton. *Now Discover Your Strengths.* New York: Free Press, 2001.

Clifton, Donald O. and E. Anderson. *Strengths Quest: Discover and Develop Your Strengths in Academics, Career, and Beyond.* Washington, DC: The Gallup Organization, 2002.

Kalil, Carolyn. *Follow Your True Colors to the Work You Love.* Corona, CA: True Colors, 1998.

Miscisin, Mary. *Showing Our True Colors.* Riverside, CA: True Colors Publishing, 2001.

Myers, Isabel B. and M. H. McCaulley. *Manual: A Guide to the Development and Use of the Myers-Briggs Indicator.* Palo Alto, CA: Consulting Psychologists Press, 1985.

Group Development

Jacobs, Ed E., Robert L. Masson, and Riley L. Harvill. *Group Counseling: Strategies and Skills.* 5th ed. Belmont, CA: Thomson Brooks/Cole, 2006.
Johnson, David W. and Frank P. Johnson. *Joining Together: Group Theory and Group Skills.* 9th ed. Boston: Pearson Education, Inc., 2006.
Weaver, Richard G. and John D. Farrell. *Managers as Facilitators.* San Francisco: Berrett-Koehler Publishers, Inc., 1997.

CHAPTER 3: FACILITATING INSPIRATIONAL ENVIRONMENTS

Engaging Employees

BlessingWhite. *The Organizational Dance Card: A BlessingWhite Survey Report on Employee Engagement.* Princeton, NJ: BlessingWhite, Inc., 2004.
Clifton, C. and G. Gonzalez-Molina. *Follow This Path: How the World's Greatest Organizations Drive Growth by Utilizing Human Potential.* New York: Warner Books, 2002.
Quinn, Robert E., Sue R. Faerman, Michael P. Thompson, and Michael R. McGrath. *Becoming a Master Manager.* New York: John Wiley and Sons, Inc., 1990.
Shenkman, Michael E. *The Strategic Heart.* Westport, CT: Quorum Books, 1996.

CHAPTER 4: FACILITATING COLLABORATIVE DECISION MAKING

Managing Change

Lawson, E. and C. Price. "The Psychology of Change Management." *The McKinsey Quarterly.* Available from http//:www.mckinseyquarterly.com/ 2003.
Prochaska, J. O. "How Do People Change, and How Can We Change to Help Many More People?" In *The Heart and Soul of Change*, eds. M. Hubble, B. L. Duncan, and S. Miller, 227–58. Washington, DC: American Psychological Association, 2003.

Decision-Making Strategies and Styles

Heller, Frank, ed. *Managing Democratic Organizations.* Brookfield, VT: Ashgate, 2000.

Shenkman, Michael E. *The Strategic Heart.* Westport, CT: Quorum Books, 1996.

CHAPTER 5: FACILITATING COMMUNICATION AND CONFLICT RESOLUTION

Communication Skills

Frey, Lawrence R., ed. *New Directions in Group Communication.* Thousand Oaks, CA: SAGE Publications, 2002.

Schwartz, Roger M. *The Skilled Facilitator: A Comprehensive Resource for Consultants, Facilitators, Managers, Trainers, and Coaches.* 2nd ed. San Francisco: Jossey-Bass, 2002.

Conflict Resolution

Fisher, Erik A. and Steven W. Sharp. *The Art of Managing Everyday Conflict: Understanding Emotions and Power Struggles.* Westport, CT: Praeger, 2004.

Huffington, Clare, ed. *Working Below the Surface: The Emotional Side of Contemporary Organizations.* New York: Karnac, 2004.

Lipsky, David B., Ronald L. Seeber, and Richard D. Fincher. *Emerging Systems for Managing Workplace Conflict: Lessons From American Corporations for Managers and Dispute Resolution Professionals.* San Francisco: Jossey-Bass, 2003.

CHAPTER 6: FACILITATING WORK SESSIONS

Planning for Successful Work Sessions

Streibel, Barbara J. *The Manager's Guide to Effective Meetings.* New York: McGraw-Hill, 2003.

Tropman, John E. *Effective Meetings: Improving Group Decision Making.* 2nd ed. Thousand Oaks, CA: SAGE Publications, 1996.

Group-Facilitation Skills

Jacobs, Ed E., Robert L. Masson, and Riley L. Harvill. *Group Counseling: Strategies and Skills.* 5th ed. Belmont, CA: Thomson Brooks/Cole, 2006.

Johnson, David W. and Frank P. Johnson. *Joining Together: Group Theory and Group Skills.* 9th ed. Boston: Pearson Education, Inc., 2006.

Kottler, Jeffrey A. *Learning Group Leadership: An Experiential Approach.* Boston: Allyn and Bacon, 2001.

Balancing Process and Task Functions

Corey, Marianne Schneider and Gerald Corey. *Groups: Process and Practice.* 7th ed. Belmont, CA: Thomson Brooks/Cole, 2006.
Hulse-Killacky, Diana, Jim Killacky, and Jeremiah Donigian. *Making Task Groups Work in Your World.* Upper Saddle River, NJ: Prentice-Hall, Inc., 2001.

CHAPTER 7: FACILITATING DIVERSITY

Beamer. Linda and Iris Varner. *Intercultural Communication in the Global Workplace.* New York: McGraw-Hill/Irwin, 2001.
Mor-Barak, Michalle E. *Managing Diversity: Toward a Globally Inclusive Workplace.* Thousand Oaks, CA: SAGE Publications, 2005.
Phatak, Arvind V., Rabi S. Bhagat, and Roger J. Kashlak. *International Management: Managing in a Diverse and Dynamic Global Environment.* Boston: McGraw-Hill/Irwin, 2005.
Plummer, Deborah L., ed. *Handbook of Diversity Management: Beyond Awareness to Competency Based Learning.* Lanham, MD: University Press of America, 2003.
Trompenaars, Fons and Charles Hampden-Turner. *Managing People Across Cultures.* Padstow, Cornwall, England: T.J. International Ltd., 2004.

Notes

Introduction

1. Marcus Buckingham and Curt Coffman, *First, Break All the Rule* (New York: Simon & Schuster, 1999), p. 11.
2. Ibid., p. 235.
3. Thomas Stewart, *Intellectual Capital* (New York: Doubleday, 1999), p. 51.

Chapter 1

1. Michael H., Shenkman, *The Strategic Heart* (Westport, CT: Quorum Books, 1996), p. 82.
2. Marcus Buckingham and Curt Coffman, *First, Break All the Rules* (New York, Simon & Schuster, 1999), pp. 238–42.
3. C. Honoré, *In Praise of Slowness: How a Worldwide Movement is Challenging the Cult of Speed* (San Francisco: Harper, 2004), pp. 34–39.
4. E. Diener and M. Seligman, "Beyond Money," *Psychological Science in the Public Interest*, 5, no. 1 (2004), pp. 1–31.

Chapter 2

1. Max De Pree, *Leading Without Power: Finding Hope in Serving Community* (San Francisco: Jossey-Bass, 1997), p. 63.

2. Richard G. Weaver and John D. Farrell, *Managers as Facilitators* (San Francisco: Berrett-Koehler Publishers, Inc., 1997), pp. 40–41.

3. Robert E. Quinn, Sue R. Faerman, Michael P. Thompson, and Michael R. McGrath, *Becoming a Master Manager* (New York: John Wiley & Sons, 1990), p. 200.

4. Weaver and Farrell, pp. 26–36.

Chapter 3

1. Michael E. Shenkman, *The Strategic Heart* (Westport, CT: Quorum Books, 1996), pp. xii–xiii.

2. John Heron, *The Complete Facilitator's Handbook* (Sterling, VA: Stylus Publishing, 1999), p. 347.

3. Robert E. Quinn, Sue R. Faerman, Michael P. Thompson, and Michael R. McGrath, *Becoming A Master Manager: A Competency Framework* (New York: John Wiley & Sons, 1990), pp. 55–57.

4. Ibid., p. 56.

Chapter 4

1. Robert E. Quinn, Sue R. Faerman, Michael P. Thompson, and Michael R. McGrath, *Becoming a Master Manager* (New York: John Wiley & Sons, 1999), p. 211.

2. Ibid., p. 212.

3. Victor H. Vroom and Philip W. Yetton, *Leadership and Decision-Making* (Pittsburgh, PA: University of Pittsburgh, 1973), pp. 47–51.

4. Michael E. Shenkman, *The Strategic Heart* (Westport, CT: Quorum Books, 1996), p. 31.

Chapter 5

1. Robert E. Quinn, Sue R. Faerman, Michael P. Thompson, and Michael R. McGrath, *Becoming a Master Manager* (New York: John Wiley & Sons, 1999), p. 224.

2. Ibid., pp. 179–80.

3. Ibid., pp. 225–26.

Chapter 6

1. Ed E. Jacobs, Robert L. Masson, and Riley L. Harvill, *Group Counseling: Strategies and Skills*, 5th ed. (Belmont, CA: Thomson Brooks/Cole, 2006), p. 20.
2. Ibid., p. 51.
3. Diana Hulse-Killacky, Jim Killacky, and Jeremiah Donigian, *Making Task Groups Work in Your World* (Upper Saddle River, NJ: Prentice-Hall, 2001), p. 9.

Chapter 7

1. Linda Beamer and Iris Varner, *Intercultural Communication in the Global Workplace* (New York: McGraw-Hill/Irwin, 2001), p. xv.
2. Rich Feller and Judy Whichard, *Knowledge Nomads and the Nervously Employed: Workplace Change and Courageous Career Choices* (Austin, TX: CAPS Press, 2005), p. 31.
3. Linda Beamer and Iris Varner, *Intercultural Communication in the Global Workplace* (New York: McGraw-Hill/Irwin, 2001), p. 3.
4. LaRay M. Barna, "Stumbling Blocks in Intercultural Communication," in *Intercultural Communication: A Reader*, 4th ed., ed. Larry A. Samovar and Richard E. Porter (Belmont, CA: Wadsworth Publishing Company, 1985), pp. 330–37.

Chapter 8

1. Robert E. Quinn, Sue R. Faerman, Michael P. Thompson, and Michael R. McGrath, *Becoming a Master Manager* (New York: John Wiley & Sons, Inc. 1990), p. 320.

Index

About the Authors

JUDY WHICHARD is President of Consulting Associates, an educational consulting firm specializing in diversity. She is a former international banker, inner city teacher, high school principal, and assistant professor at Colorado State University. She is coauthor of *Knowledge Nomads and the Nervously Employed*, as well as many articles on presentations on facilitation, educational policy and reform, training, and diversity.

NATHALIE L. KEES is Associate Professor in the Counseling and Career Development Program, Colorado State University, where she teaches courses in counseling, diversity, and educational psychology. A Licensed Professional Counselor, she also runs a private practice and has served as a group facilitator, trainer, and consultant to school districts, universities, government agencies, non-profits, and businesses. She has published dozens of articles in such publications as the *Journal of Counseling and Development* and the *Journal for Specialists in Group Work*, and has served on a variety of task forces promoting diversity.